MRS. B. RICH
THORPE SATCHVILLE
MELTON MOWBRAY
LEICESTERSHIRE
LE14 2DF

MY HUNTING WORLD

Jim Meads in action at a foxhound show.

MY HUNTING WORLD

Jim Meads

Quiller Press

To my wife, Pauline, who is still putting up with me and my work after 43 years of married life.

First published 1999 by
Quiller Press Ltd, 46 Lillie Road, London, SW6 1TN

ISBN 1 899163 53 0

Designed by Jo Lee
Printed by Colorcraft Ltd. Hong Kong

CONTENTS

CONTENTS

FOREWORD

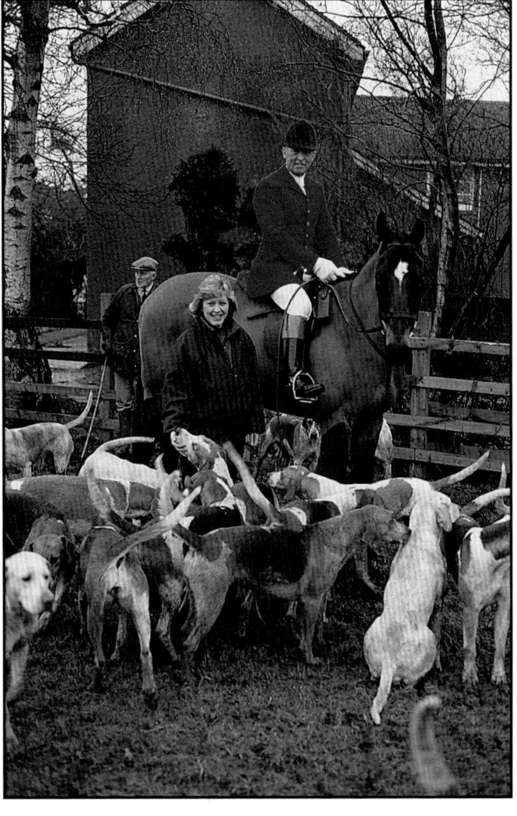

It is a tremendous honour for me to write a few lines about Jim Meads for his latest book. I have known him since 1960 when I was whipping-in at the North Cotswold to Captain Parry.

Not only is he a wonderfully gifted photographer but he is also a great personal and trusted friend of mine and very many other professional hunt servants, in all parts of the hunting world.

I have a great respect for Jim's sheer grit and determination; whether he is at a puppy show, hound show or in the hunting field, he is always the first person we all see. His ability to read a hunt and be in the right place to take such remarkable photographs amazes us all. I know when comparing notes with other huntsmen, when hounds check, he has often put us right.

Jim sometimes drives hundreds of miles to a meet, runs all day over the most difficult terrain (trainers heavy with mud) and then has to face the long journey home.

I could compare him to a hunting encyclopaedia, or 'Meads Bailys'; his knowledge of people is incredible. He knows who is going where on May 1st and all about their previous careers and never hesitates to fill us in with the changes. One could say he has a photographic memory!

It is easy to pick Jim out even several fields away. His fitness and stamina still astonishes us all, which must be a tribute to Pauline's care and attention.

I will always be grateful to him for giving me so many photographs which will give me much pleasure in the future.

Rarely have we met a man so single-minded in his dedication to his job. Well done Jim, you are a legend in your time and long may you continue to be so.

Michael Farrin.

Michael Farrin

FOREWORD

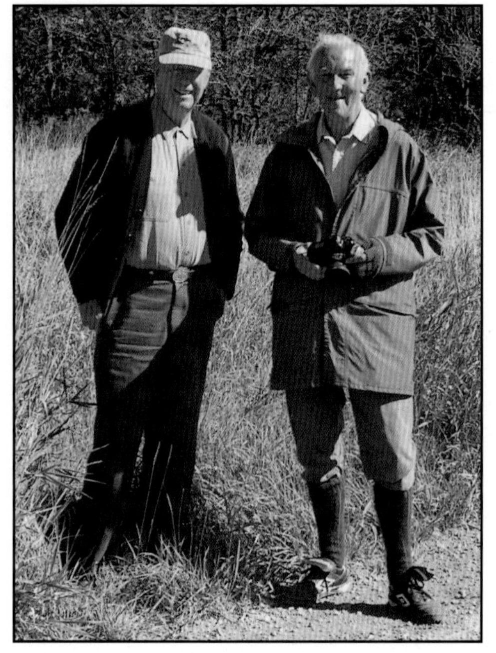

My Hunting World, what an appropriate title for Jim Meads's latest documentary on foxhunting! It's foxhunting seen, not from the back of a horse, but from nearer the elevation of fox and hound. Jim's perspective is from his two fleet feet as he runs with the hunting pack, cutting corners and taking all obstacles, in stride, to be always where the action is.

Jim is truly good at his job because: he is an extraordinary photographer, he is super physically fit, hunting is his life and, most important, the people involved in all aspects of hunting with hounds love and respect him and are honoured to have him record their sport.

My friendship with Jim goes back twenty-one years to September 1978 when I picked him up in Lexington, Kentucky after the World Championship Three Day Competition and flew him to Midland, Georgia. He was to take pictures for an article 'Hunting in Rattlesnake Country with the Midland Foxhounds' that was to appear in *Horse and Hound*'s Foxford's Hunting Diary.

It was hot, even for September in Georgia. Hounds did run very early in the morning, but when Jim disappeared into the slash pine forest at Cedar Heights, I never expected him to arrive at the earth within seconds after the hounds were marking. Later at Fitzpatrick, where we had a fair point, I was even more amazed when he showed up in the middle of a soy bean field, where hounds had checked.

Wherever there is a happening in the world of foxhunting; hound shows, puppy shows, hound competitions, special meets, ordinary meets, Hyde Park Rally July 10th, the Great Country March, The 1998 Ontario Festival of Hunting, Jim is there with his camera.

Great Britain, the USA and Canada are on his regular beat and he can be relied on to report the hunting news.

These foxhunting happenings around the world are skilfully presented to the public via *Horse and Hound* in Jim's 'Hunting World' section. It's the very first section I turn to on receiving my copy. His written accounts of these events are every bit as artfully recorded as the pictures that accompany them.

This latest child of Jim's unique talent will be a must for foxhunters on both sides of the Atlantic.

Good hunting Jim.

Benjamin H. Hardaway

Benjamin H Hardaway III MFH

INTRODUCTION

I was born on 9 July 1930, in Hertfordshire, a few miles North of London, the first son of Sports and Gardens photographer Frank Meads. Five years later we moved to a house in the country and at once I found myself in my true environment, spending all my spare time in woods and fields, learning about nature from hands-on experiences. I also learned to ride, becoming a member of the Enfield Chace Pony Club, foxhunting with that pack as often as money allowed. When I was eleven I was fortunate enough to win a scholarship from Essendon Village School, to Hertford Grammar School, which meant a 6-mile cycle ride each way, 6 days a week; good for the legs and lungs! Here my teachers made me knuckle down to work and encouraged me to play cricket, so successfully that I later made it into the school's First XI.

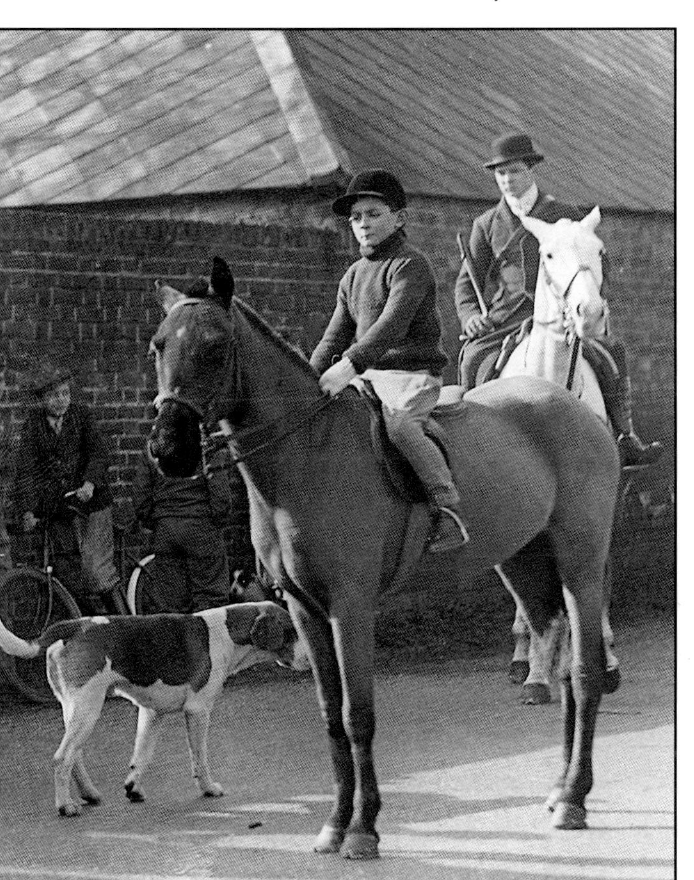

Out with the Enfield Chace Hunt in 1938.

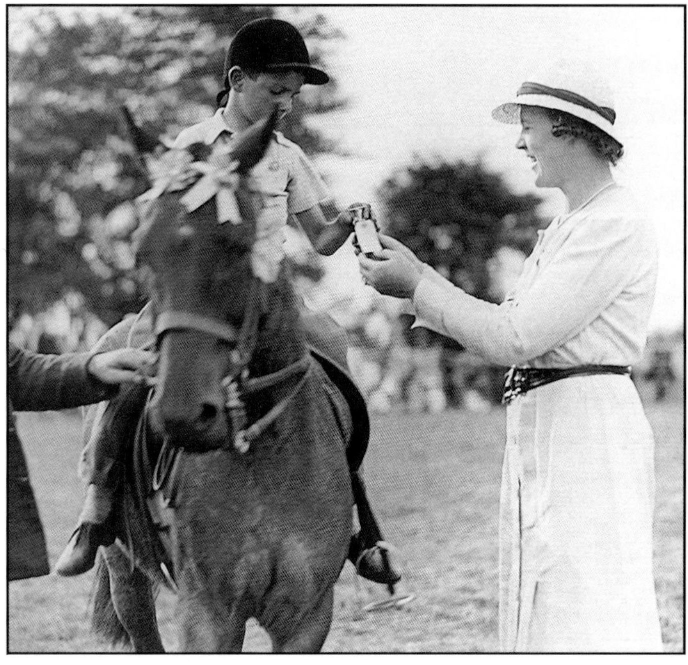

Receiving a gymkhana cup from Mrs Trotter in 1939.

A slight hiccup occurred on 1 July 1944 when a flying bomb blew our house down on top of us, luckily at 5.30 am, so we were in bed asleep, thus escaping serious injury. In the school holidays I cycled all over England staying in Youth Hostels and taking photos of steam locomotives in stations and out in the country. Fortunately there were not as many vehicles on the roads as there are today, so cycling was a far less hazardous pastime than in 1999.

Leaving school the minute I was 16, the Headmaster's parting words were, "The cricket team will miss you!" Immediately I became a trainee photographer at the De Havilland Aircraft Company which still meant cycling 6 miles each way as money was in short supply, my weekly wage being £2.50! Luckily I had Saturdays and Sundays free so I was able to go out with packs of hounds near home, with my camera, endeavouring to produce interesting action photos, yet still with pleasing countryside backgrounds. It wasn't long before I came to realise that the only way to achieve this was by leaving the roads and crossing the country as fast as possible on foot, however strenuous and tiring this proved to be. So the 'running photographer legend' began! I have always been a quick learner and try never to make the same mistake twice, so at De Havillands it wasn't long before I was flying with many famous wartime pilots, photographing one aeroplane from another, flying in close formation; all exciting stuff for a teenager who loved aircraft. In addition I was learning all I could about hunting on my Saturday forays, although this was to come to a halt in November 1948, when I became Aircraftsman Meads JR, spending an enjoyable 18 months in the Royal Air Force. I had always dreamed of being a fighter pilot, but there were so many left over from the war, as with photographers, that I became a lorry driver instead. This was great as I was out and about all the time, seeing more and more of our country and yet I was still able to take my leave to coincide with the Peterborough Royal Foxhound Show. De-mobbed on 1 May 1950, a significant date in hunt service, I became a self-employed sports photographer and

After running 8 miles with the York and Ainsty (South) Hunt near Huby (Yorkshire). Jan 22nd 1957.

immediately began trying to save enough money to buy a motor cycle, as this would be much less expensive to purchase and run than a car. Soon I was spreading my wings, venturing further and further afield, while photographing hunting, and now point to point racing as well. I started regularly to have pictures published in *Horse and Hound* and was making just enough money to keep the wolf from the door, although more was needed in 1956 when I married Pauline and again when our sons Paul and Barry arrived on the scene! Sadly neither of them was interested enough in later life to follow in my footsteps and become a sporting photojournalist!

In 1958 Sir Andrew Horsbrugh-Porter became hunting correspondent to *The Field* and he and I formed a partnership which endured for 13 marvellous seasons, until Sir Andrew's retirement in 1971. People have always said that I am very 'lucky' and I'm more than happy to go along with that statement, but on 13 September 1962 Lady Luck really did look on me most favourably. On that Friday afternoon I was baby-sitting my two sons and took them to Hatfield aerodrome, where I had worked from 1946-48, to watch aeroplanes taking off and landing. For some inexplicable reason I took a camera along with me, something I never do unless I'm working. As we watched a Lightning jet fighter coming in to land something went wrong and the plane went into a vertical dive, at very low altitude, while the pilot left the cockpit in his ejector seat. The ensuing photo was voted 'Picture of the Year 1962' and I was 'famous' for a few days

About to take off for an aerial photographic sortie in a Tiger Moth, 1955.

With his first hunting camera, 1950.

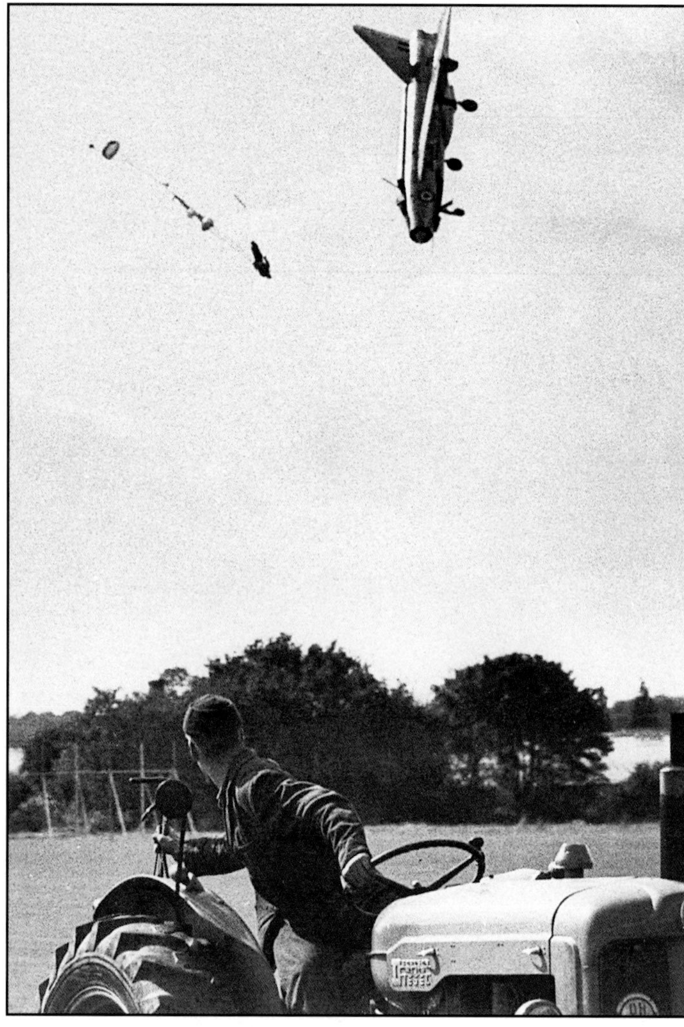

'Picture of the year' 1962.

1970 brought an invitation from *Shooting Times and Country Magazine* to write and illustrate a weekly series for them on hunting, racing, shooting and fishing, again in many parts of the world. This contract was to last until 1984 when a change in policy led to them dropping all mention of hunting. However, in 1973 my great friend Michael Clayton was appointed Editor of *Horse and Hound* and began the most popular 'Foxford's Hunting Diary'. For the next 23 years we had a splendid partnership, with Michael writing the stories and me taking the pictures. Indeed, on one memorable occasion we arrived at a meet of the Cheshire Hunt to be greeted by the words, "I see we have the A-team out with us today"! In 1975, encouraged by the many Americans I had met in the UK, I, greatly daring, booked myself onto a plane and made my first visit to the USA. I was overwhelmed by their kindness and hospitality and even now,

Working in pouring rain, at the Dublin Horse Show, in the 1970s.

and of course the cheque was a big boost to our finances!

During the terrible winter of 1962-63, when hunting in the UK was stopped by deep snow, I made my debut in Ireland and really felt that I had 'arrived' on the fox-hunting scene, now that I had travelled overseas. Some 5 years later I began to photograph horse trials and over the years went on many interesting trips to major events including Kentucky in 1978; France in 1980; Switzerland in 1981; Germany in 1982 and, most exciting of all, to Gawler, South Australia in 1986.

after some 75 return crossings of the Atlantic, I still get an enormous 'buzz' each time I go to America.

19th February 1977 was a red letter day for me, as well as a nerve-wracking one, for on that day I was privileged and honoured to meet HRH Prince Charles for the first time and photograph him in his revived Windsor livery, out with the Cottesmore Hunt. Since then I have become one of his most loyal supporters and have taken pictures of him many times, often jumping huge obstacles, as he rides at the head of affairs, close behind the huntsman, who is blazing the trail.

Lady Luck was again much in evidence on 25 November 1978 when Foxford and I were visiting the Tanatside Hunt in Montgomeryshire. Hounds were in full cry, with the mounted field in hot pursuit, while I was running as fast as I could to keep in touch. It seems that one of the tail end riders came very close to me and as she passed, her horse lashed out sideways, kicking me in the face and knocking me out for the count. I woke up in a Land Rover *en route* for Welshpool hospital, yet still holding on to my camera, as someone so kindly said, "With a dead man's grip"! With stitches inserted close to my left eye and in my badly gashed chin and my broken nose straightened, I tried to regain my composure before discharging myself and obtaining a lift back to where the hunt was still taking place. I continued taking photos until 'Home' was blown as I didn't want to lose my nerve, for being on foot amongst horses!

November 1979 saw the publication of my book *They Still Meet at Eleven* with a foreword by Michael Clayton, which proved a great success. Throughout the 1980s life continued in the usual hectic fashion, with hunting, hound shows,

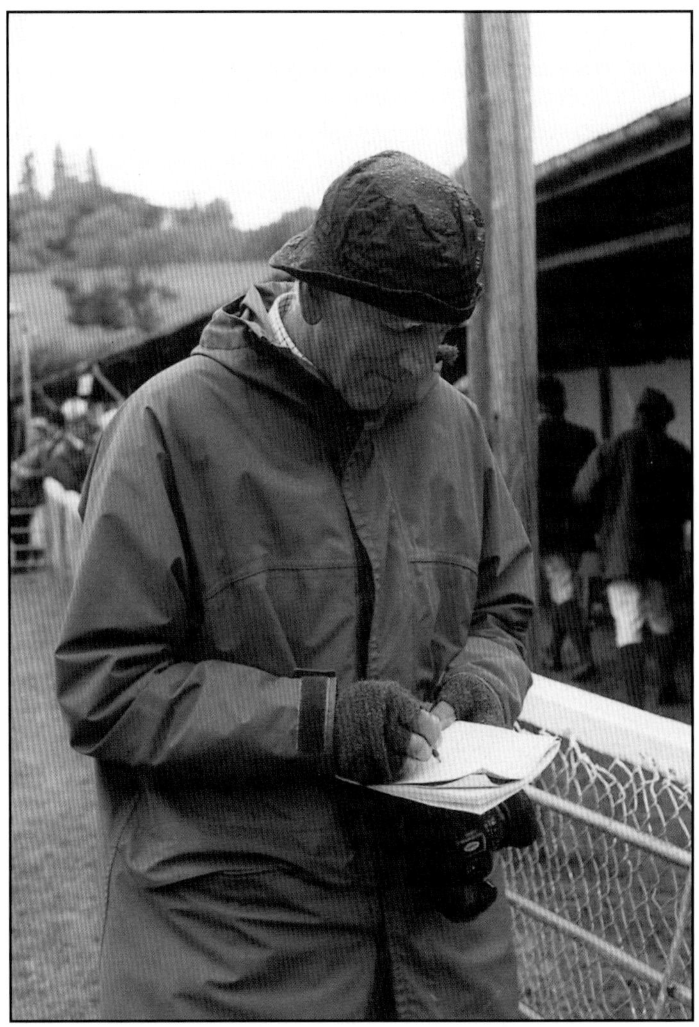

At a very wet Welsh Hound Show.

point to points, 3 day events and shooting, filling my diary. In November 1991 I had published *They Will Always Meet at Eleven* and I deemed it a great honour to have the foreword penned by HRH Prince Charles. The following month found me in Virginia for the great foxhound match between the home pack, the Piedmont, hunted by the very professional Randy Waterman MFH, and the visiting Midland hounds from Georgia, cheered on in exuberant fashion by the famous Ben Hardaway III MFH. This event took place over 7 days and it was a real pleasure and privilege to take tea on several evenings with

America's former First Lady and dedicated foxhunter, Jacqueline Kennedy Onassis. She graciously accepted a copy of *They Will Always Meet at Eleven* and I greatly treasure a handwritten letter from Mrs Onassis, expressing her thanks for the book and her astonishment at the speed I crossed the country on foot. 17th July 1996 was another red-letter day, which happened completely out of the blue, at the Peterborough Royal Foxhound Show. Called into the ring by the show president, Lt Col Sir John Miller, as I thought, to take a photo, I was overwhelmed to be presented with a fantastic painting by the very talented artist Joy Hawken, of myself photographing a champion hound at Peterborough. This was to commemorate my 50th year at the show and the money for the painting was donated by the hunt servants of the world. Unemotional though I am, tears still trickled down my blushing cheeks!

Six weeks later I was appointed a weekly columnist to *Horse and Hound* writing Jim Meads Hunting World. However, on 7th November 1996 Lady Luck once again came to my rescue. Flying with *Horse and Hound's* new Editor Arnold Garvey, *en route* to Kentucky, to do a feature on the Iroquois Hunt, our MDII aircraft developed a problem. For 90 minutes we circled Cincinnati, practising the 'crash position', until an announcement said that we had permission to divert to Wright-Patterson airforce base, Dayton, Ohio, where there was a 5-mile long runway. With brilliant airmanship the pilots put us down safely, landing at '300 mph' before stopping close to the end of the runway amidst a wild burst of cheering from the relieved passengers, and surrounded by squads of firemen in flame-proof overalls. Our excitement was still not over as we were given the order "One minute to evacuate the aircraft", as a tornado was coming our way! It missed!

1 May 1999 marked the beginning of my 50th year as the 'running photographer' and to date I have been out with, and photographed 437 different packs of hounds; a world record! To commemorate this landmark and to take hunting into the new millennium, I decided to produce a book of colour pictures entitled *My Hunting World*, with forewords by great friends and huntsmen from both sides of the Atlantic – Ben Hardaway III MFH of the Midland Hunt in Georgia and Alabama since 1950, and Michael Farrin, who hunted the Quorn hounds in High Leicestershire so brilliantly for 30 magical seasons.

Since 1950, when I began my job with a very old-fashioned plate camera, things have changed dramatically. The countryside, climate, fashions in farming, politics and travel are all vastly different, as we reach the year 2000. However, fox hunting, hare hunting, stag hunting and in America, coyote hunting go from strength to strength, giving tremendous pleasure to tens of thousands of ordinary people. Long may it continue, so that new generations of people can thrill to the sound of the horn and hounds in full cry, in pursuit of their natural quarry in their natural environment, despite man's attempt to spoil it.

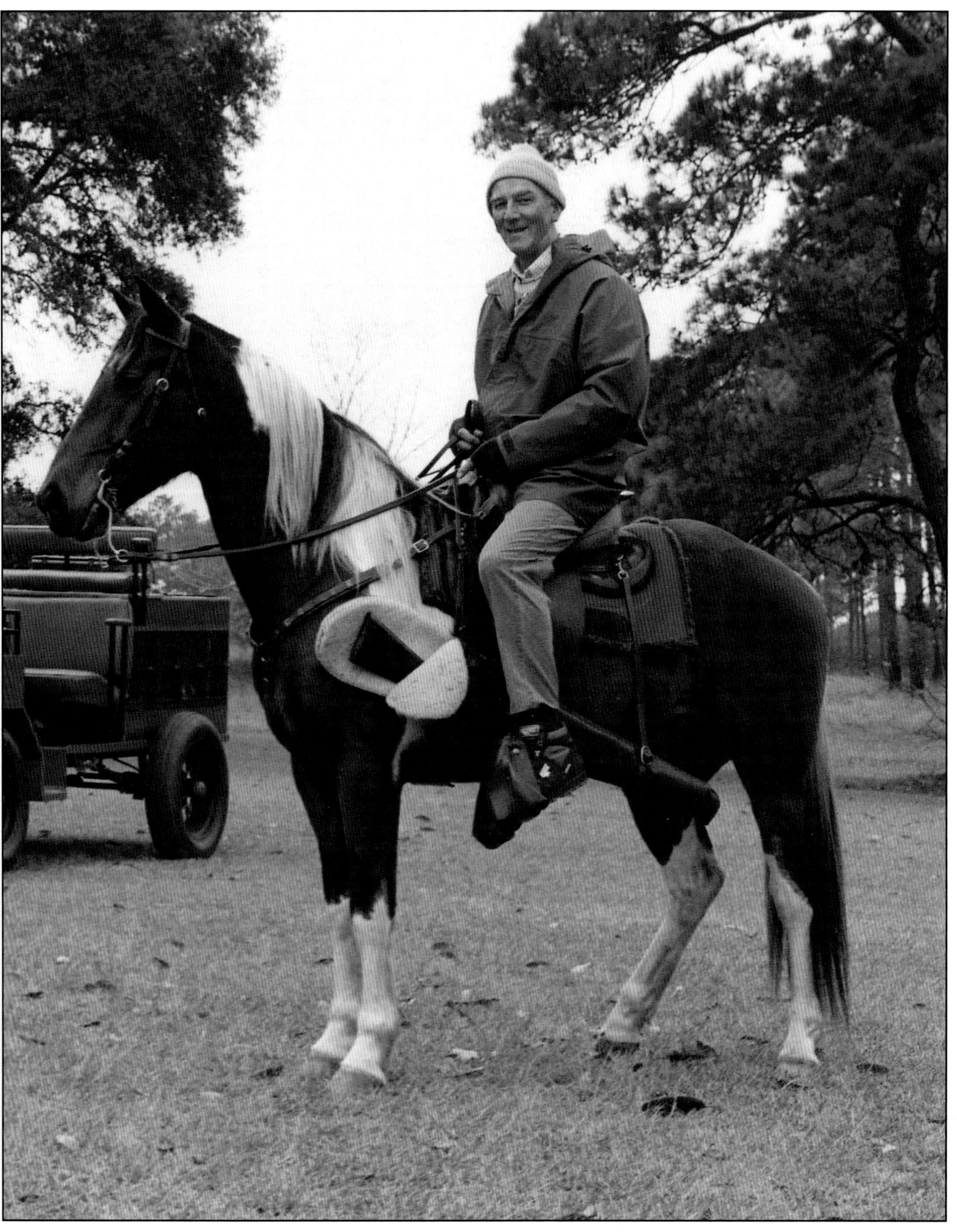

Riding a Tennessee walking horse on the Merrily Quail shooting plantation in Georgia, U S A.

This splendid painting by Joy Hawken was presented to Jim Meads by 'The Hunt Servants of the World' to commemorate his 50 years at the Peterborough Royal Foxhound Show.

MY HUNTING WORLD

The BANWEN MINERS *Hunt* (SOUTH WALES)

Banwen Miners joint master Chris Davies in full flight over a stone and earth bank, more often found in Ireland than South Wales.

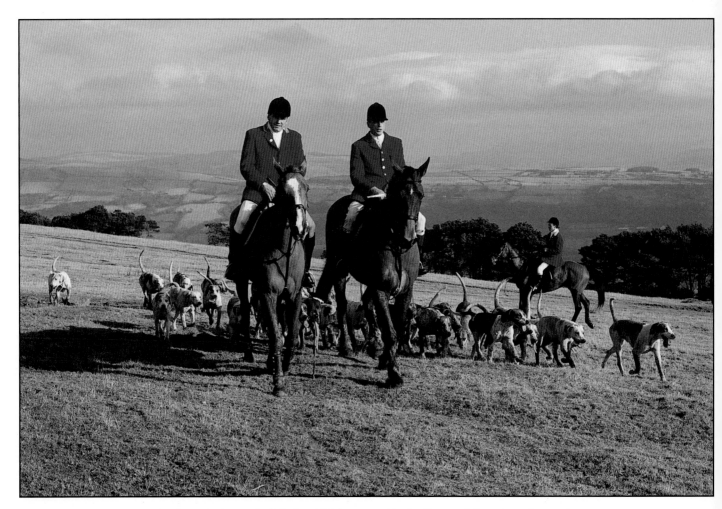

Against a background of glorious Welsh countryside, the Banwen Miners hounds are taken to draw by retiring huntsman Anthony Edwards and (right) his successor Phillip Leech. This hunt was formed in 1962 and centred on the tiny coal mining village of Banwen.

The Duke of
BEAUFORT'S
Hunt
(GLOUCESTERSHIRE AND WILTSHIRE)

The Duke of Beaufort's hounds, led by kennel-huntsman Charles Wheeler, leaving the kennels for a walk in Badminton Park.

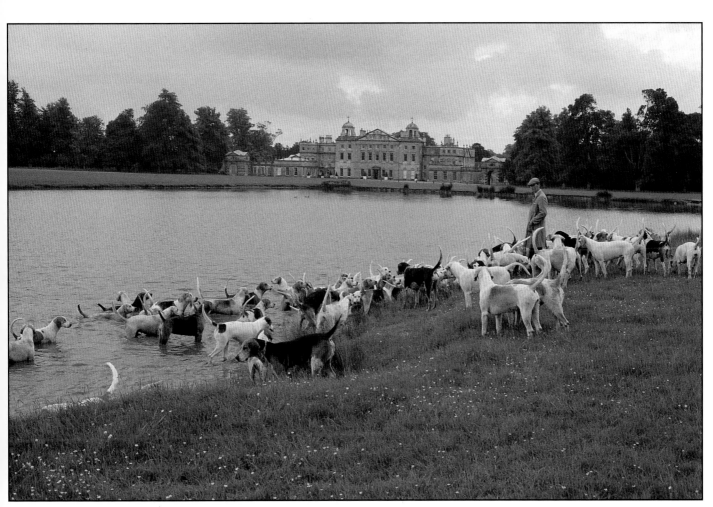

With Badminton House in the background, the Duke of Beaufort's hounds enjoy themselves in the lake, made famous by the 3-day event. The hunt has been in existence for more than 200 years.

B

The
BEAVER MEADOW
Hunt
(CANADA)

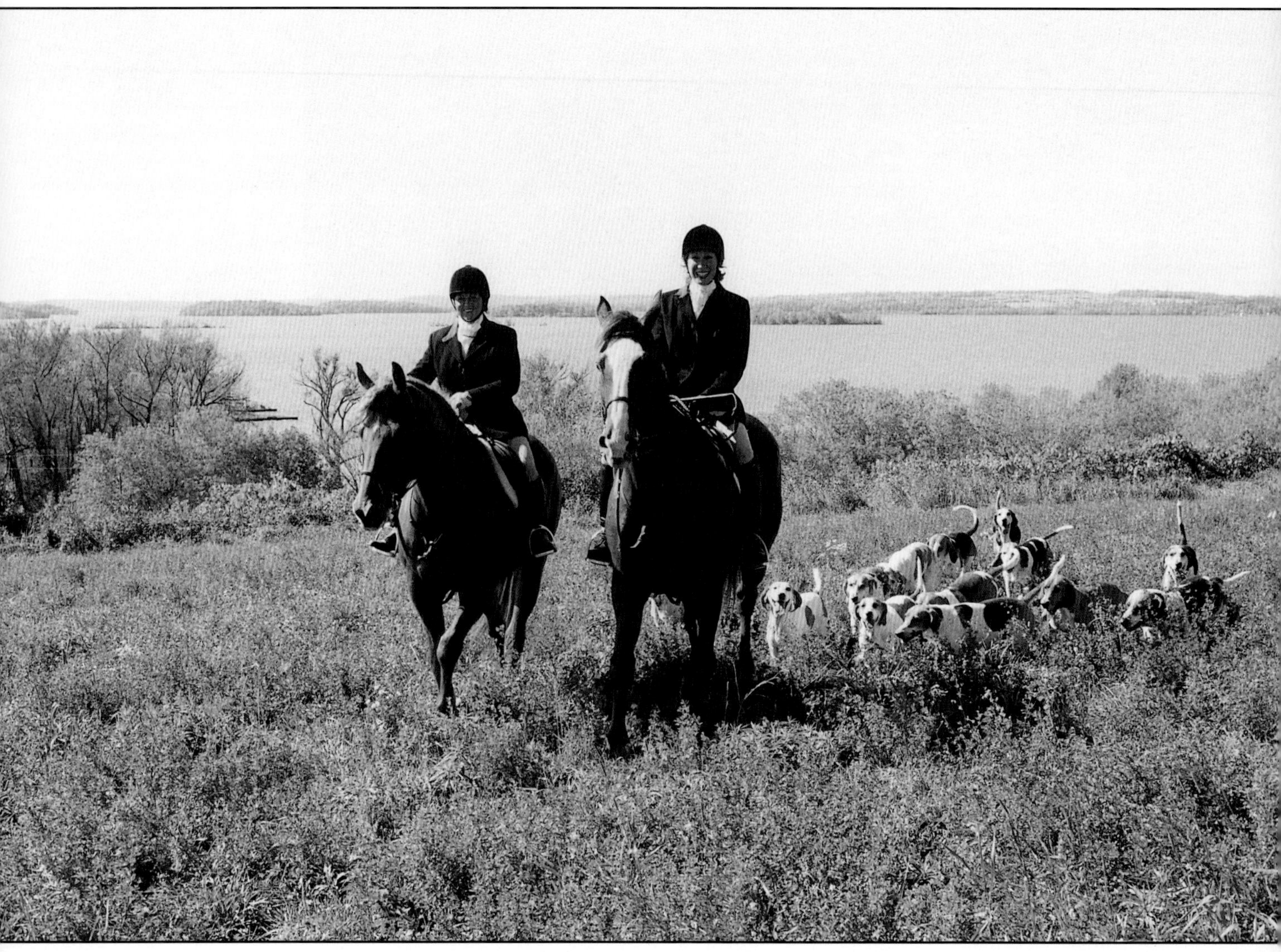

The joint masters of Canada's newest foxhunt, Olga Chernuck and (left) Gayle Killoran, with the Beaver Meadow hounds, against a background of Rice Lake and close to the hunt kennels.

The BELLE MEADE *Hunt* (UNITED STATES OF AMERICA)

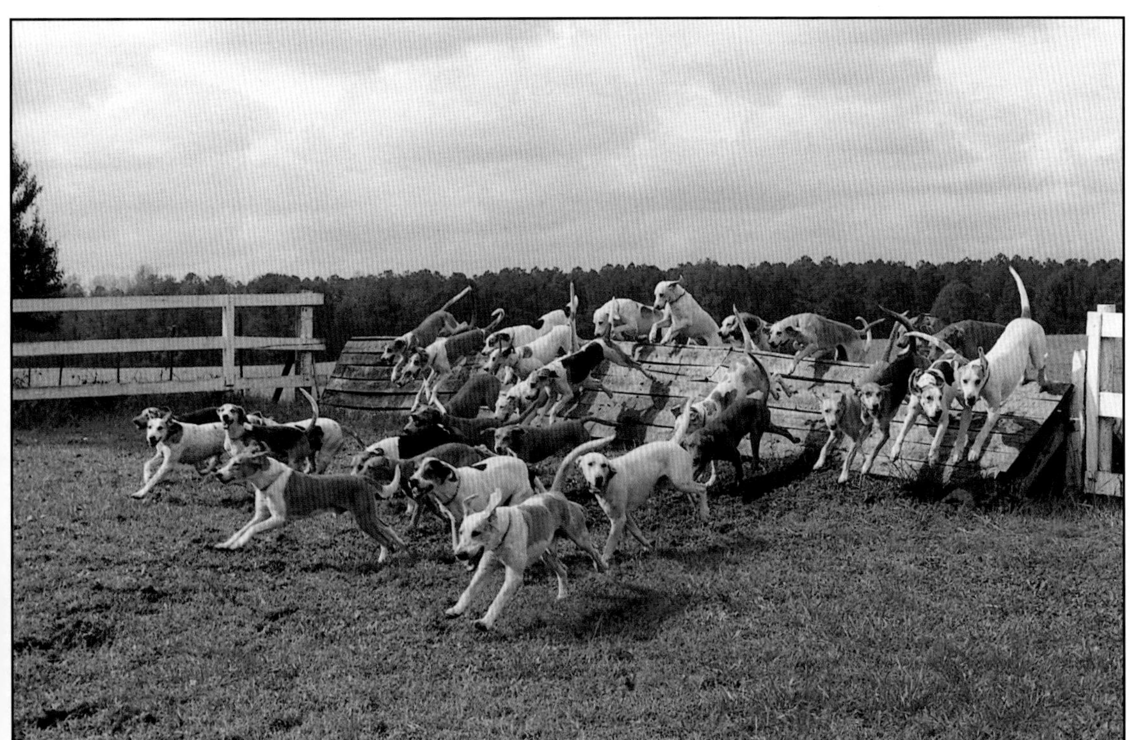

Hounds of the Belle Meade Hunt in Georgia, joyously jumping a wide coop, following the opening meet and hound blessing.

The Belle Meade hounds, led by joint master and huntsman 'Epp' Wilson, and his whipper-in wife Sharon, coming in at the end of their opening meet hunt. This is normally attended by more than 100 riders and several hundred others who travel on a series of 'Tally-Ho wagons'.

B

The
BELVOIR
Hunt
(LEICESTERSHIRE AND LINCOLNSHIRE)

Belvoir huntsman Martin Thornton collecting his Old English hounds, after drawing a covert blank, much to his dismay.

The end of day, as Belvoir huntsman Martin Thornton prepares to box up his pack of Old English hounds. These are owned by the Duke of Rutland as are the large kennels, close to Belvoir Castle.

The BERKELEY *Hunt* (GLOUCESTERSHIRE)

Lt Col Rollo Clifford MFH Berkeley Hunt leading the field over a small post and rails, during a hunt. Hounds have been kept at Berkeley since the 12th century, initially hunting the stag, but since the 18th century they have only hunted foxes.

Resplendent in his yellow livery, Berkeley huntsman Chris Maiden, whose family have been in hunt service since 1680, waiting for the points to take their place before putting his eager hounds in to draw a field of kale.

The
BERMINGHAM AND NORTH GALWAY
Hunt
(IRELAND)

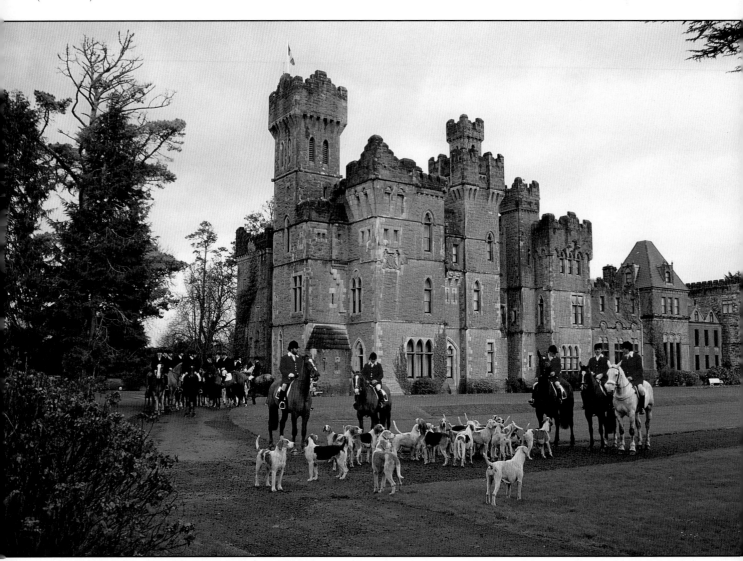

The Bermingham and North Galway Hunt makes a tremendous spectacle, as they meet at the splendid Ashford Castle Hotel.

The BICESTER WITH WHADDON CHASE *Hunt*

(OXFORDSHIRE, BUCKINGHAMSHIRE AND NORTHAMPTONSHIRE)

Bicester with Whaddon Chase huntsman Patrick Martin pops over a timber hunt jump and ditch, ahead of hounds, following a lawn meet at the home of Michael Heseltine MP. The present pack was formed in 1986 with the amalgamation of the Bicester and Warden Hill Hunt, with the Whaddon Chase.

B

The BLENCATHRA *Hunt* (CUMBRIA)

Barry Todhunter, who has hunted the Blencathra hounds since 1988, with his pack which had run a fox down from the fells, marking it to ground in a hedgerow. The Blencathra is also known as 'John Peel's Hounds' as many pedigrees go back to his pack.

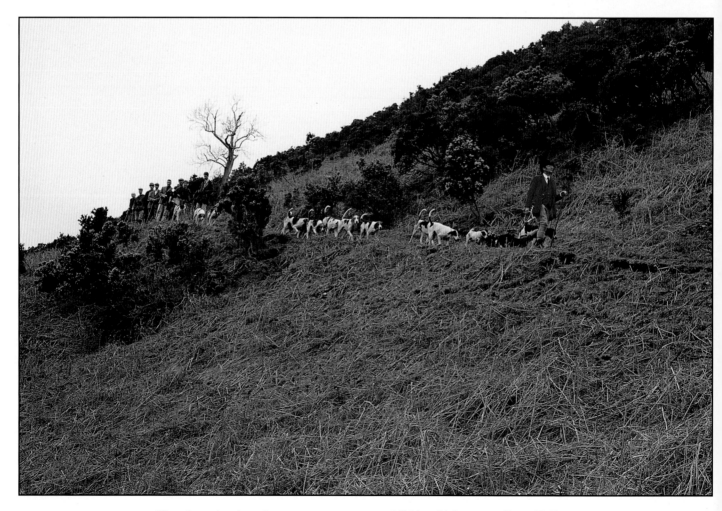

Hounds passing through a gorse covert on a steep hillside, with huntsman Barry Todhunter leading the way. Behind are some of the more energetic members of the field who climb the fells to see the hunt.

B

The BLUE RIDGE *Hunt* (UNITED STATES OF AMERICA)

The Blue Ridge hounds crossing a creek in Virginia with huntsman Chris Howells – one of the first Englishmen to take a job in hunt service in America.

Leading the hounds and a well mounted field along a typical dirt road in Virginia is English huntsman Chris Howells and long serving master Judy Greenhalgh, in charge since 1971.

B

The
BORDER COUNTIES
Hunt

The Border Counties otterhounds on the River Severn with Ray Williams, their brilliant joint master and huntsman from 1961-76.

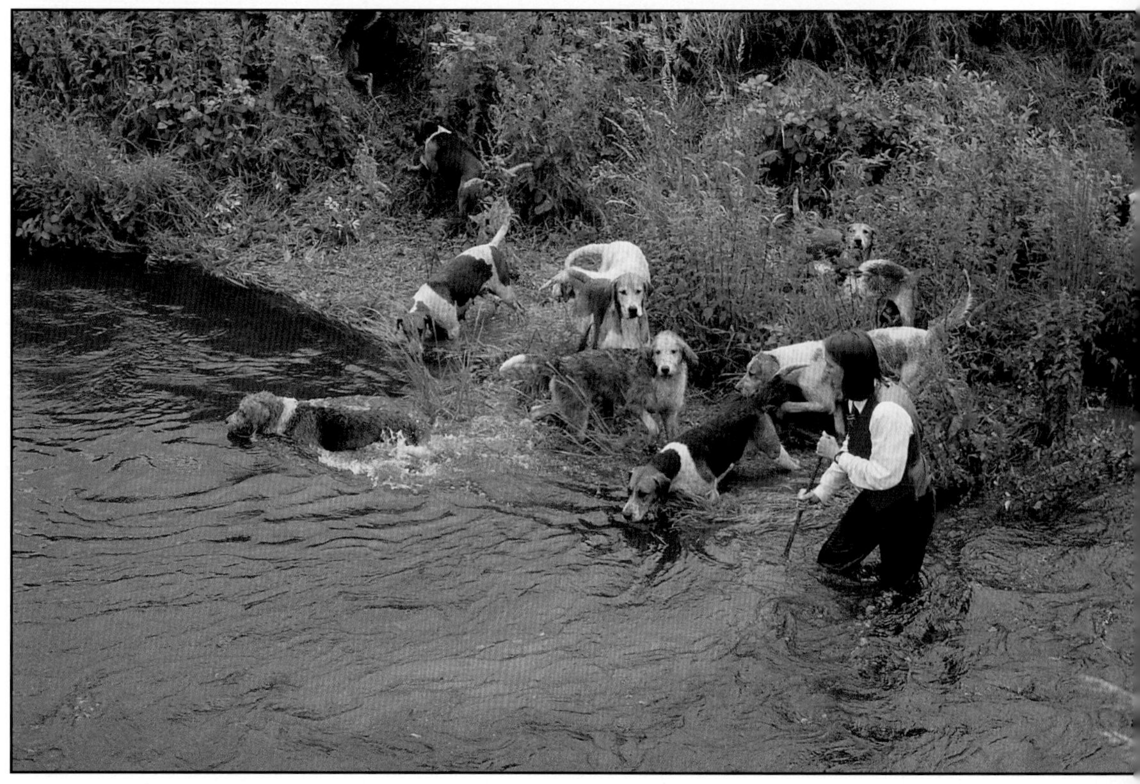

Master and huntsmen of the Border Counties mink hounds in 1998, Ruth Newton, with hounds working the River Trannon.

The BRANDYWINE *Hunt* (UNITED STATES OF AMERICA)

John White, who hunted the Brandywine hounds for 50 years, leading his pack of American hounds along a Pennsylvania lane, close to the Brandywine River.

The Duke of BUCCLEUCH'S *Hunt* (SCOTLAND)

The Duke of Buccleuch's hounds and the Jedforest hounds being taken across the River Ale by Trevor Adams MFH and Walter Jeffrey MFH, during a joint day's hunting.

The end of a splendid hunt, as the Duke of Buccleuch's hounds and the Jedforest hounds mark their fox to ground on the side of a valley.

The CAMARGO *Hunt* (United States of America)

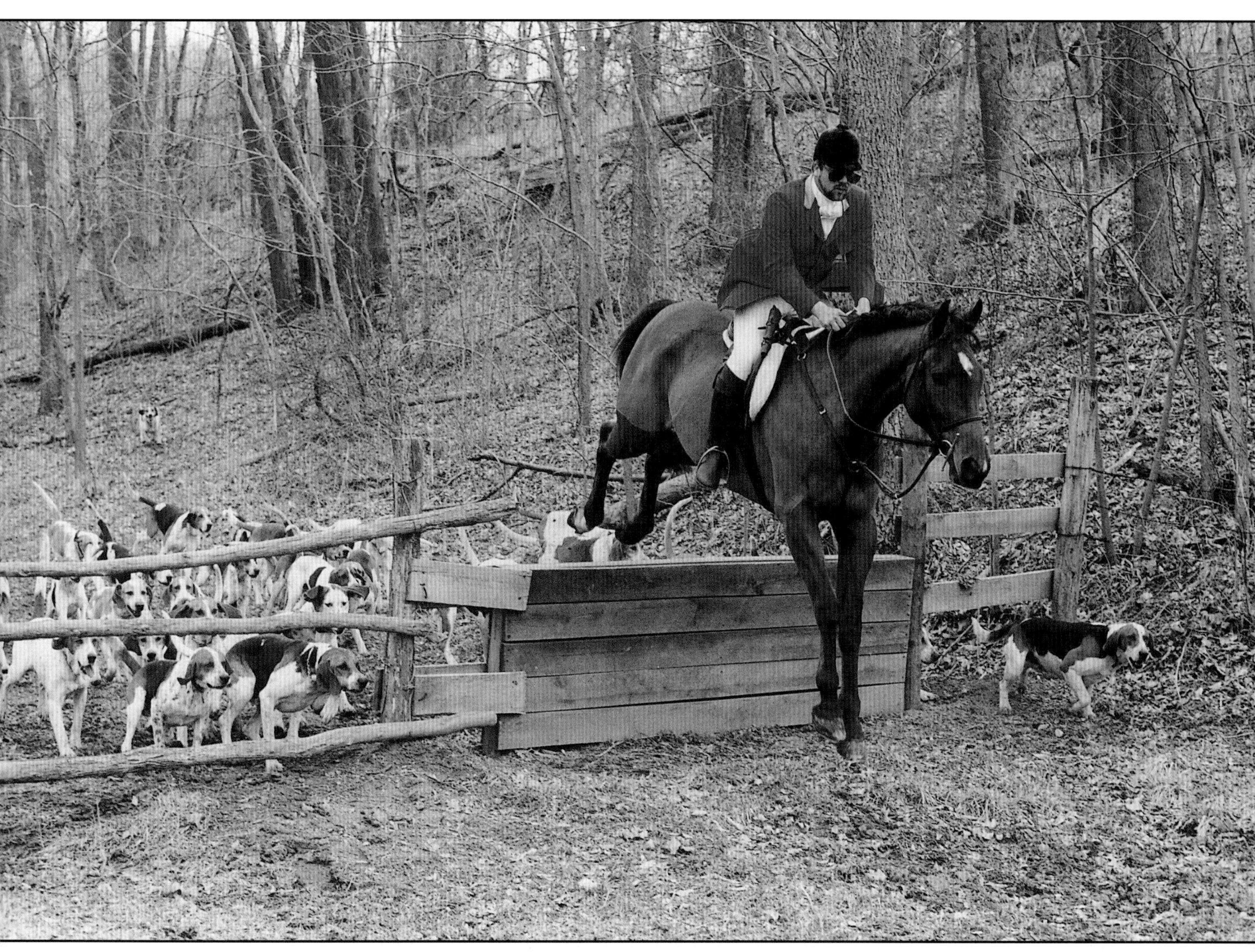

With bare woods behind, Camargo huntsman Danny Kerr jumps a coop ahead of hounds.
The Camargo Hunt has country in Southern Ohio and Northern Kentucky.

The CATTISTOCK *Hunt* (DORSET AND SOMERSET)

Cattistock huntsman Charlie Watts and hounds, with the very smartly painted kennels at Cattistock in the background.

With the Cattistock hounds, at a well attended pony club camp, are huntsman Charlie Watts and senior joint master Charlotte Townshend. This pack now has a very useful outcross of American breeding, from Ben Hardaway's Midland pack.

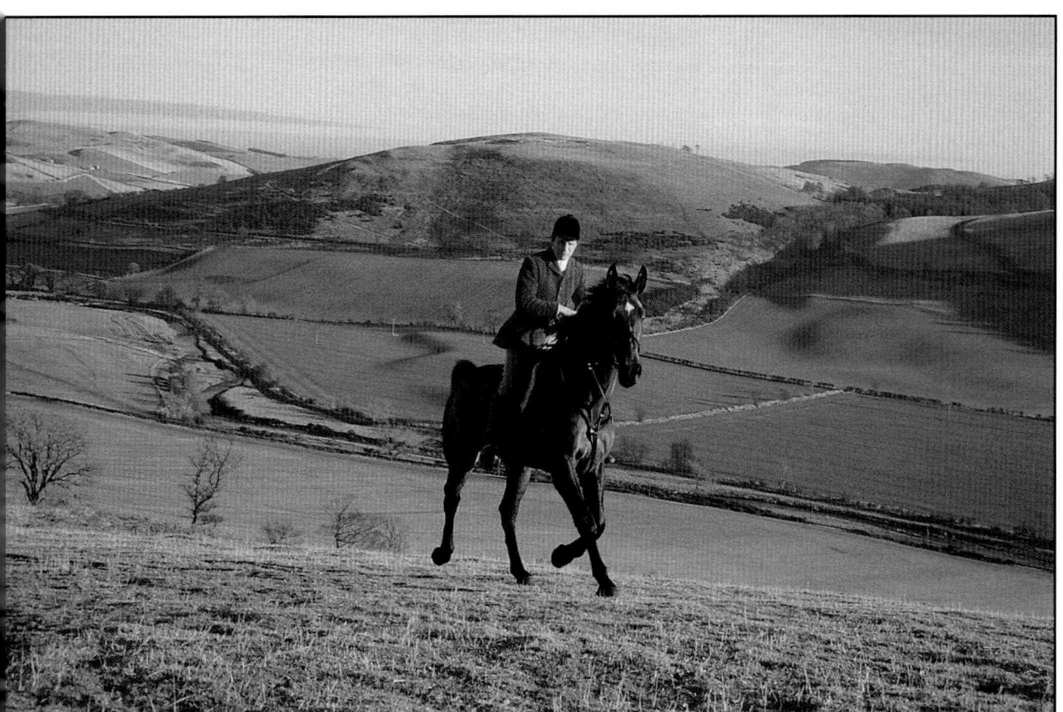

The COLLEGE VALLEY AND NORTH NORTHUMBERLAND *Hunt*

Amidst the most glorious country on the Scottish Border, College Valley kennel-huntsman Andrew Proe goes on ahead of hounds to watch for any fox which might leave, before they reach the covert.

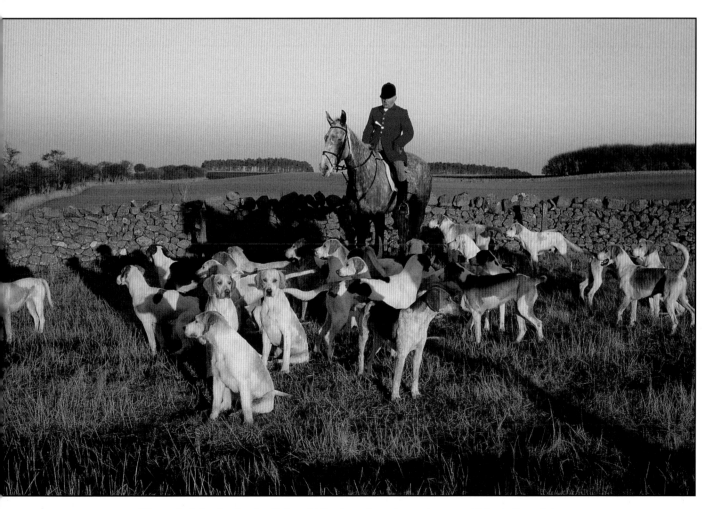

The end of the day for the College Valley hounds as they gather round Martin Letts, joint master and huntsman since 1964. On this useful day, hounds had hunted in both England and Scotland.

The COLNE VALLEY BEAGLES

Huntsman Kevin Lunn leading the Colne Valley beagles to draw, close to a babbling mountain stream.

The Colne Valley beagles in full cry across some really rugged country.

COOPS

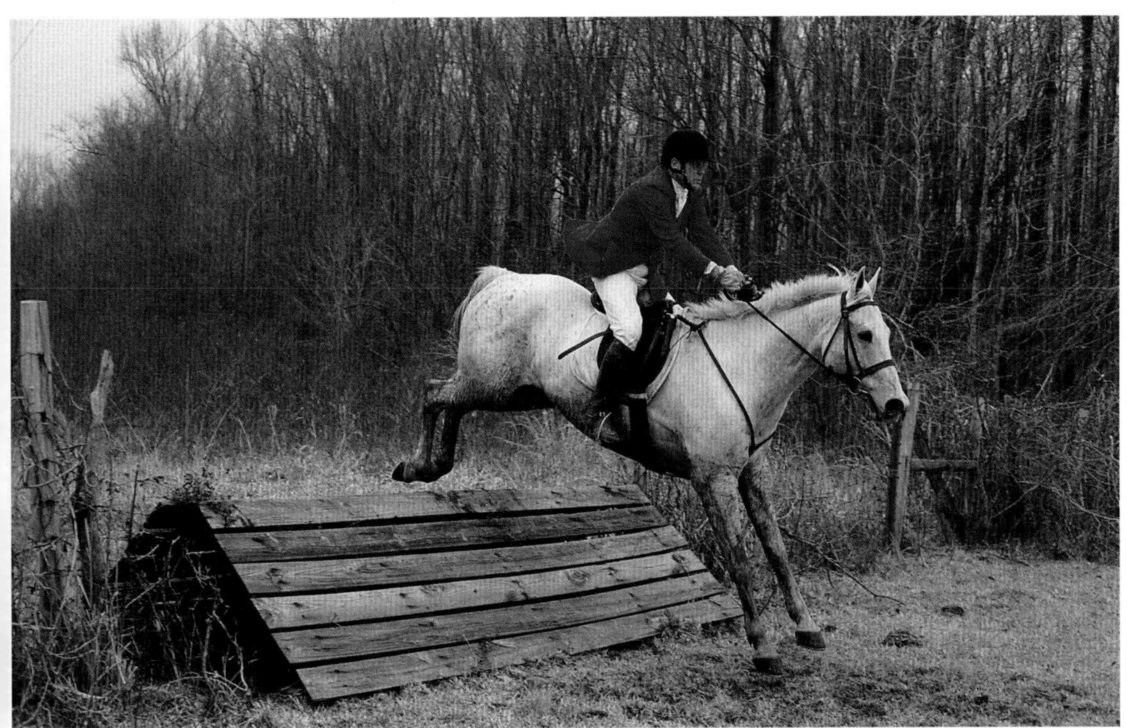

Charles Hughes, joint master and huntsman of the Whitworth hounds, over an Alabama coop.

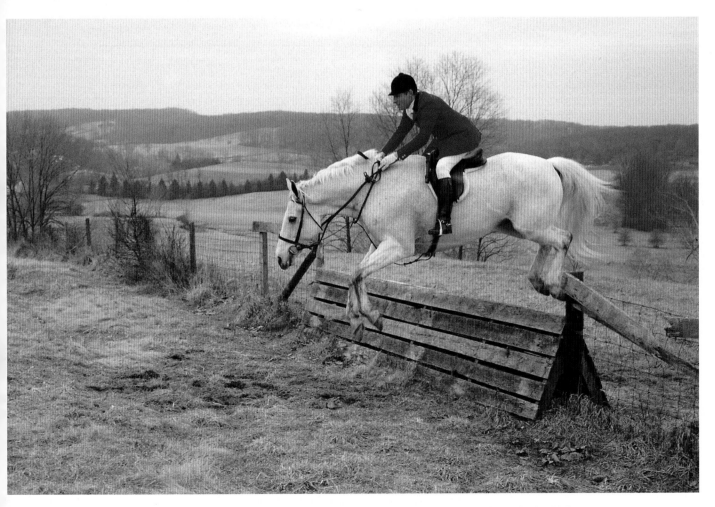

President of the American MFH Association, 'Duck' Martin, jumping a Green Spring Valley coop, of which pack he has been a master since 1977.

Cotswold kennel-huntsman from 1967-98, Roland Sheppard, hunting hounds for the last time, from his retirement meet close to Cleeve Hill, on April 1st 1998.

The COTTESMORE *Hunt* (LEICESTERSHIRE, RUTLAND AND LINCOLNSHIRE)

The Cottesmore field, on steaming horses and full of excited anticipation, moving along to watch hounds draw Ladywood covert.

The very effective Cottesmore hounds, with their huntsman Neil Coleman, moving across a big stubble field during autumn hunting. Neil has carried the horn since 1992, prior to which he was kennel-huntsman to Capt. Brian Fanshawe MFH.

C

The CUMBERLAND FARMERS *Hunt*

Tremendous support from foot followers, for the Cumberland Farmers Hunt, as joint master and huntsman Peter Wybergh takes hounds to draw, after meeting on a village green.

This pack hunts on foot, as well as on horses. Here joint master and huntsman Peter Wybergh leads his hounds to a fresh draw, followed by a large and enthusiastic field of foot followers.

The DAVID DAVIES *Hunt* (MID WALES)

This famous Welsh pack was founded in 1905 by David Davies, the first Lord Davies. Since then, only members of this family have been masters. Here, Lord Davies, in office since 1963, is seen high in the hills with his eldest daughter Eldrydd and his youngest son Ben.

Stormy weather for the David Davies Hunt, as they meet at Cider House cross-roads. With hounds are huntsman David Jones and (right) the master, Lord Davies. Not only do the David Davies have pure Welsh hounds, they also have Fell hounds, which run together most successfully.

D

The DERBY, NOTTS AND STAFFS BEAGLES

The Derby, Notts and Staffs beagles, one of the few packs which wear red coats, going to draw, on a visit to Wales. In uniform are Hon Sec Tim Hurdley, joint huntsman Marcus Wright and senior master Gerald de Ville, who owns the hounds.

Hounds hunting slowly, with joint huntsman Marcus Wright in close touch, amongst the most marvellous countryside and under a really spectacular skyscape, in mid-Wales.

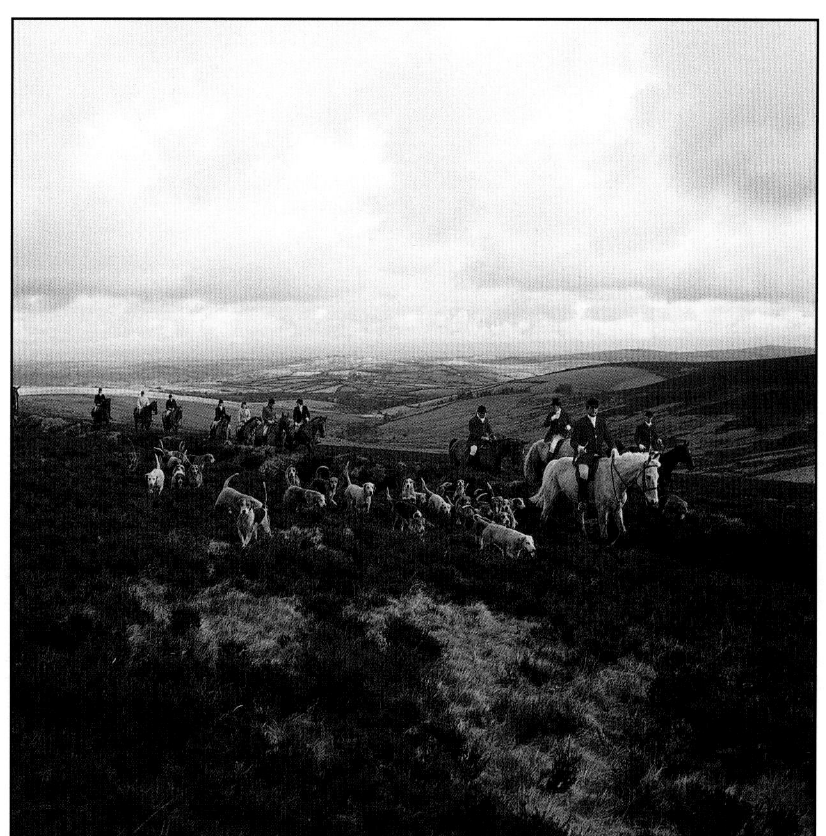

The Mid Devon's long serving huntsman Bernard Parker bringing hounds across the moor to a meet at Warren House, in pleasant conditions.

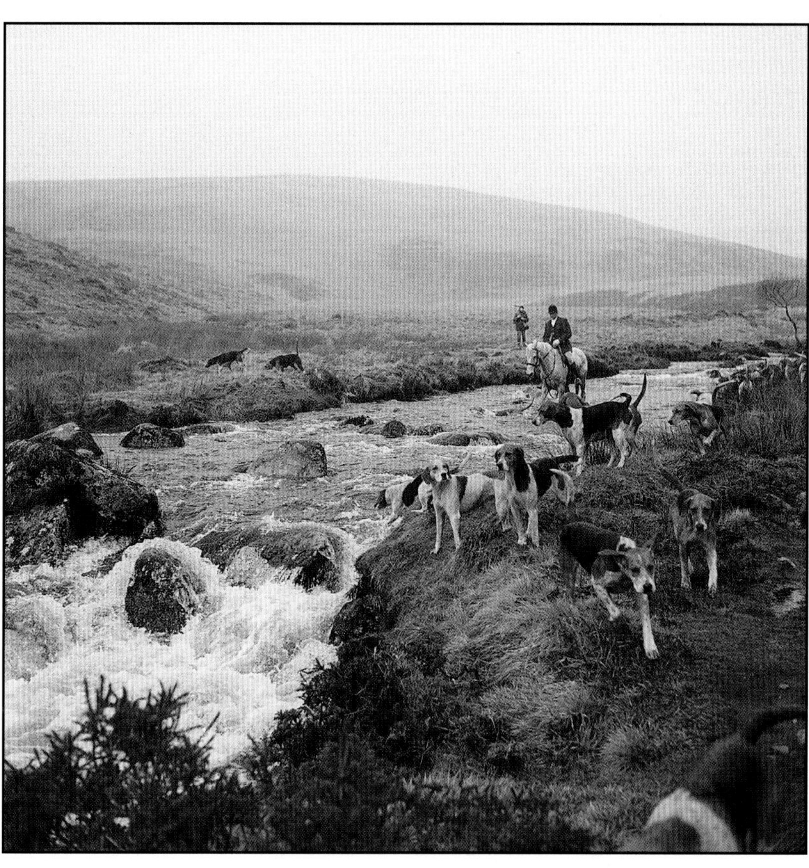

Here, later that same day, Bernard Parker is casting his hounds across the East Dart river, in torrential rain.

DITCHES

Matthew Haynes jumping an open ditch during a hunt with the Golden Vale, in Ireland.

Barlow huntsman Lindsay Hall, well over a deep, wide, open ditch

DITCHES

Johnny O'Shea, the Cheshire huntsman, takes a wet ditch in his stride, as hounds go away with a fox, in Cholmondely Park.

A Golden Vale bank and ditch, in Ireland, being cleared by Miss Lilla Mason, from Kentucky, USA, where she whips-in to the Iroquois Hunt.

DITCHES

Away

Caroline Jenks in full flight, during a good hunt with Sir Watkin Williams-Wynn's hounds.

Joint master of the North Staffordshire, Chris Mellard, going well.

DITCHES

Away

Field master to the Meynell, Phil Arthers MFH, giving a splendid lead.

David Samworth about to land well clear of a Cottesmore hedge and ditch, on his favourite grey hunter.

D

DITCHES

Towards

Di Woolley, wife of the Cheshire joint master, in action with her home pack.

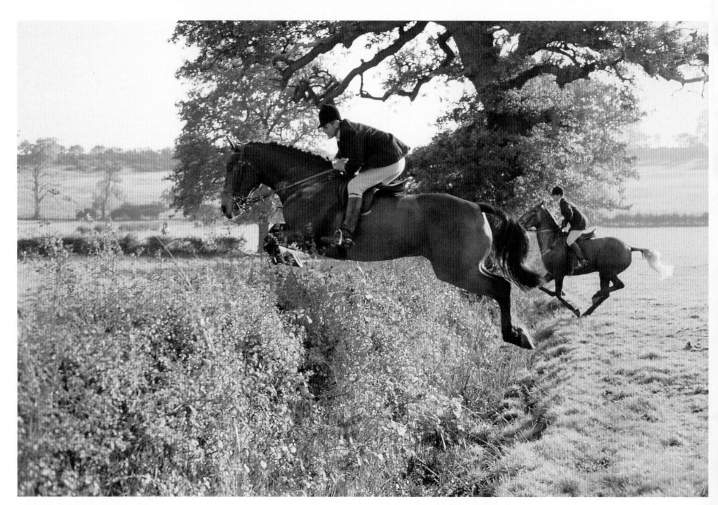

The country is still green as Tom Barlow puts in a big jump, after a Belvoir opening meet.

DITCHES

Towards

Cottesmore huntsman Neil Coleman shows how to cross the country.

Joint master and huntsman to Sir Watkin Williams-Wynn's Hunt, Robin Gundry, having made a successful cast, jumps a big ditch and hedge to keep with his hounds. Note the horn still in his hand.

D

The DULVERTON *Hunts (East and West)* (Devon and Somerset)

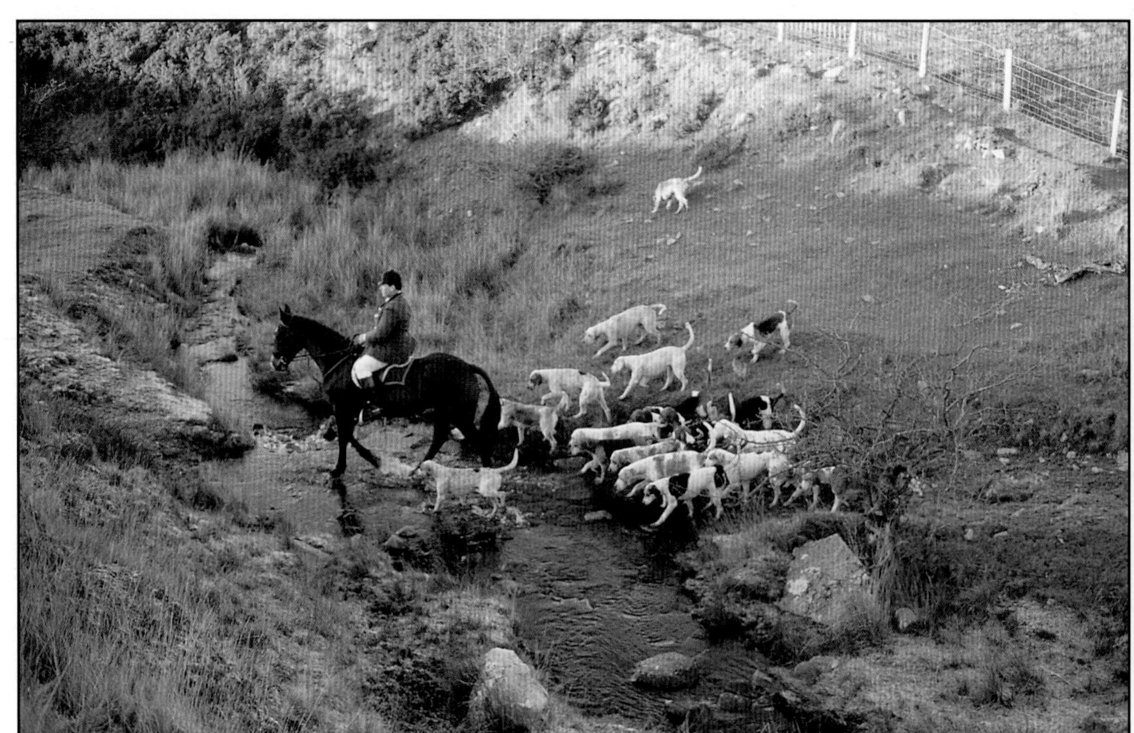

With frost still white on the grass, huntsman Anthony Allibone leads the Dulverton (East) hounds through an icy stream, on their way back to the boxes at the end of day.

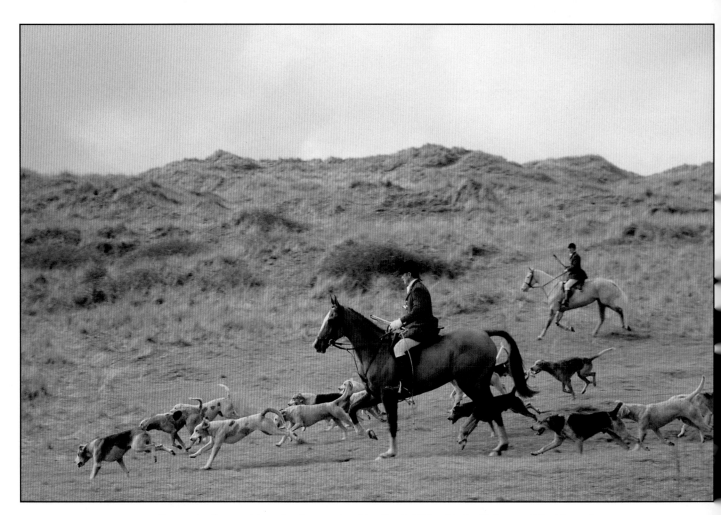

Former top horse trials and point to point rider, Bertie Hill, with the Dulverton (West) hounds on Braunton Burrows, during his 22 years term as joint master and huntsman.

The DUMFRIESSHIRE *Hunt* (SCOTLAND)

Sir Rupert Buchanan-Jardine, who has been master of the unique, black-and-tan Dumfriesshire hounds since 1950, making his way across country with his pack around him. These hounds were initially bred by Sir Rupert's father Sir John Buchanan-Jardine, who was a master from 1921-69.

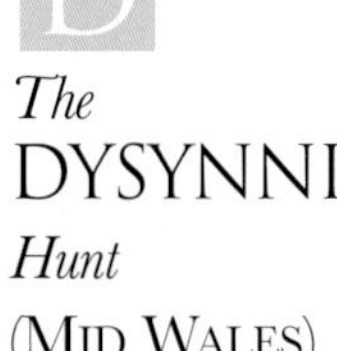

The
DYSYNNI
Hunt
(MID WALES)

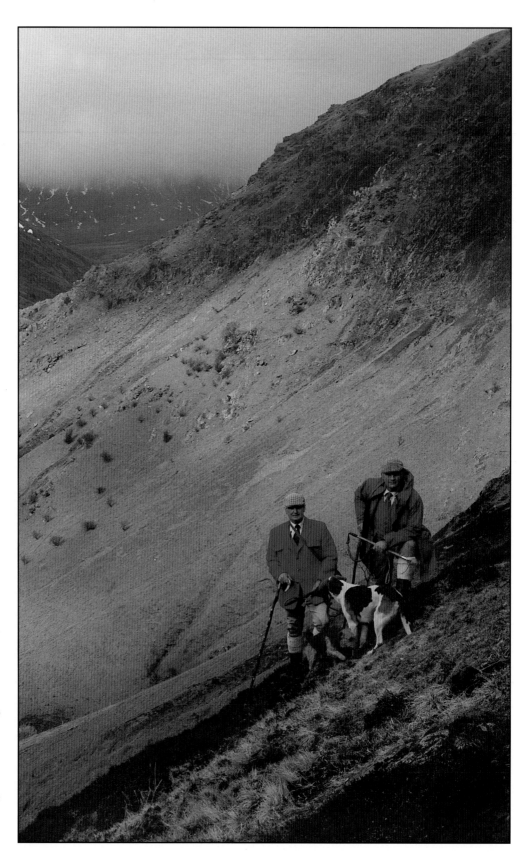

Tom Davies, master and huntsman of the Dysynni, and Jimmy Mallett, huntsman of the North Lonsdale, during a joint day in the rugged Welsh mountains. One minute earlier, a freak storm force gust of wind almost blew me into the valley, hundreds of feet below!

The EGLINTON *Hunt* (SCOTLAND)

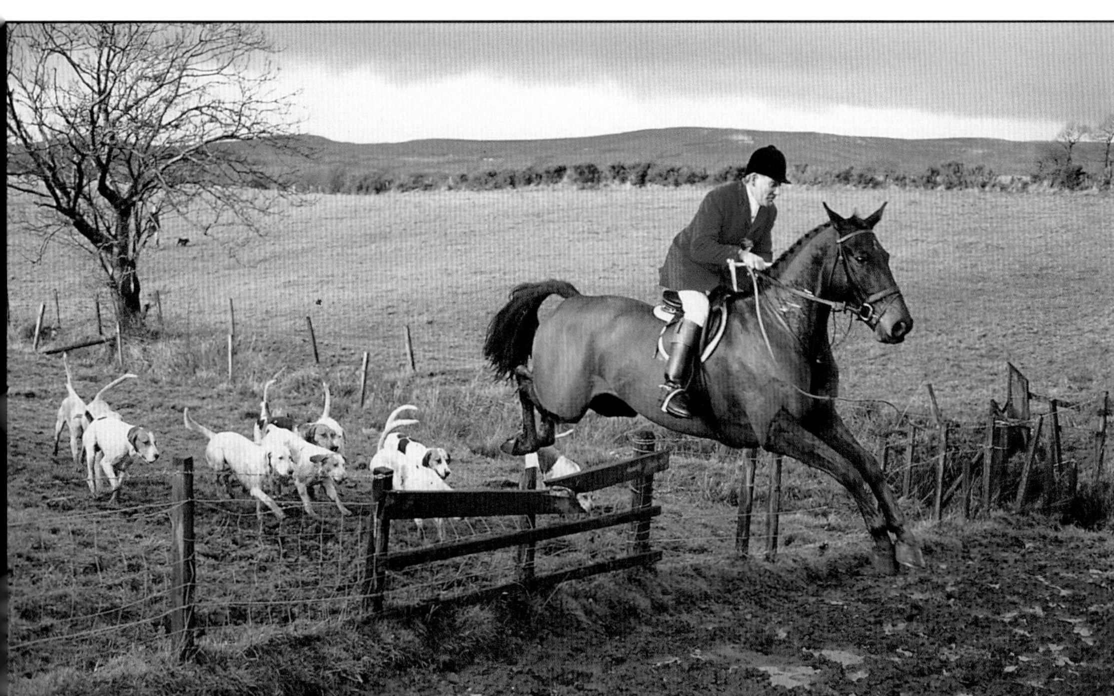

Long serving huntsman to the Eglinton, Guy Sanderson, leading hounds over a typical hunt jump

One of the great characters of foxhunting, who sadly died in 1999, the Hon Bobby Corbett MFH Eglinton Hunt, fording a stream with (left) Melvin Quarm MFH, who was one of his joint masters from 1987-94.

The
EGLINTON AND CALEDON
Hunt
(CANADA)

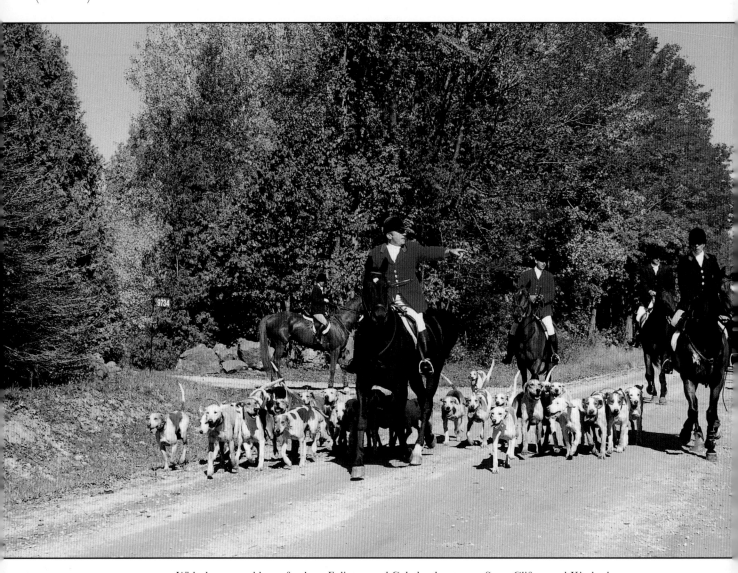

With the trees a blaze of colour, Eglinton and Caledon huntsman Steve Clifton and Kimberley Merrill take hounds to a fresh draw, in Canada.

The ELKRIDGE-HARFORD *Hunt* (UNITED STATES OF AMERICA)

Joint master of the Elkridge-Harford Hunt since 1978, Mrs John Schapiro, in action over a hunt coop.

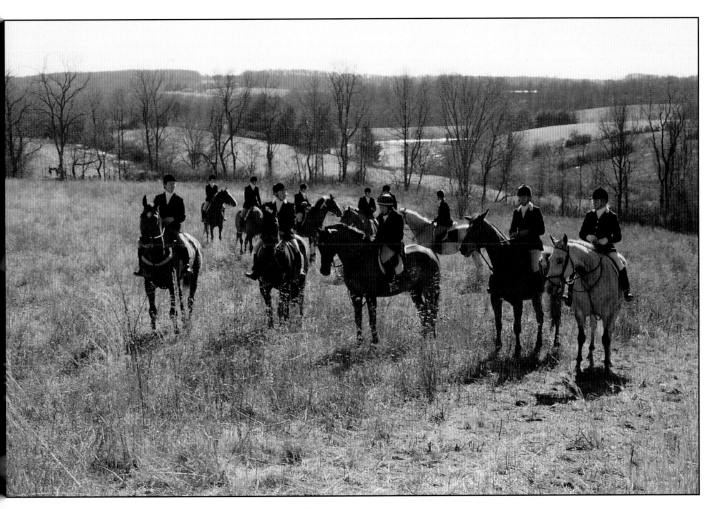

Followers of the Elkridge-Harford Hunt in Maryland watching, amongst frost burned grass, as hounds draw.

E

The
ERYRI
Hunt
(NORTH WALES)

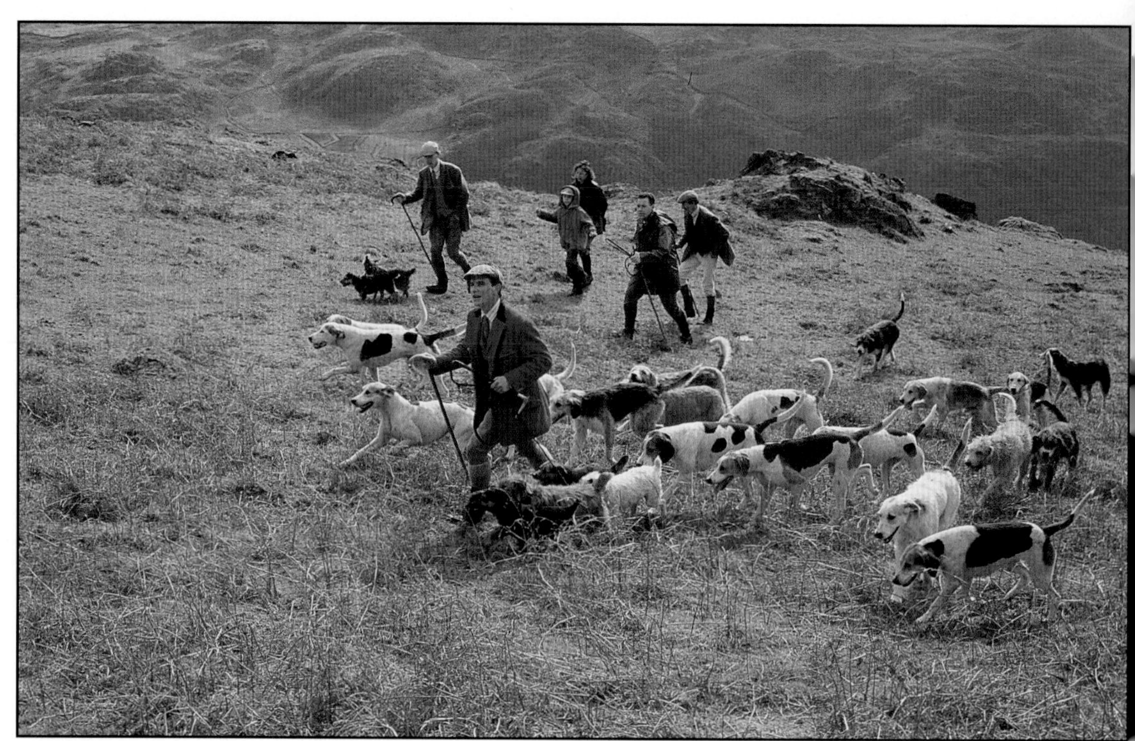

Joint master and huntsman Richard Williams, who owns the pack which was founded by his grandfather Pyrs Williams in 1968, taking hounds across country, high on the slopes of Snowdon, which peaks at 3,560 feet.

Griff Hughes, huntsman to the Eryri hounds, watching as they draw some really bleak and desolate country, close to Snowdon.

The ESKDALE AND ENNERDALE *Hunt* (CUMBRIA)

Master and huntsman Edmund Porter with his group of 5 hounds, which won the Visitors trophy at Rydal show in 1998. This was the 3rd successive year this pack had won this prestigious class.

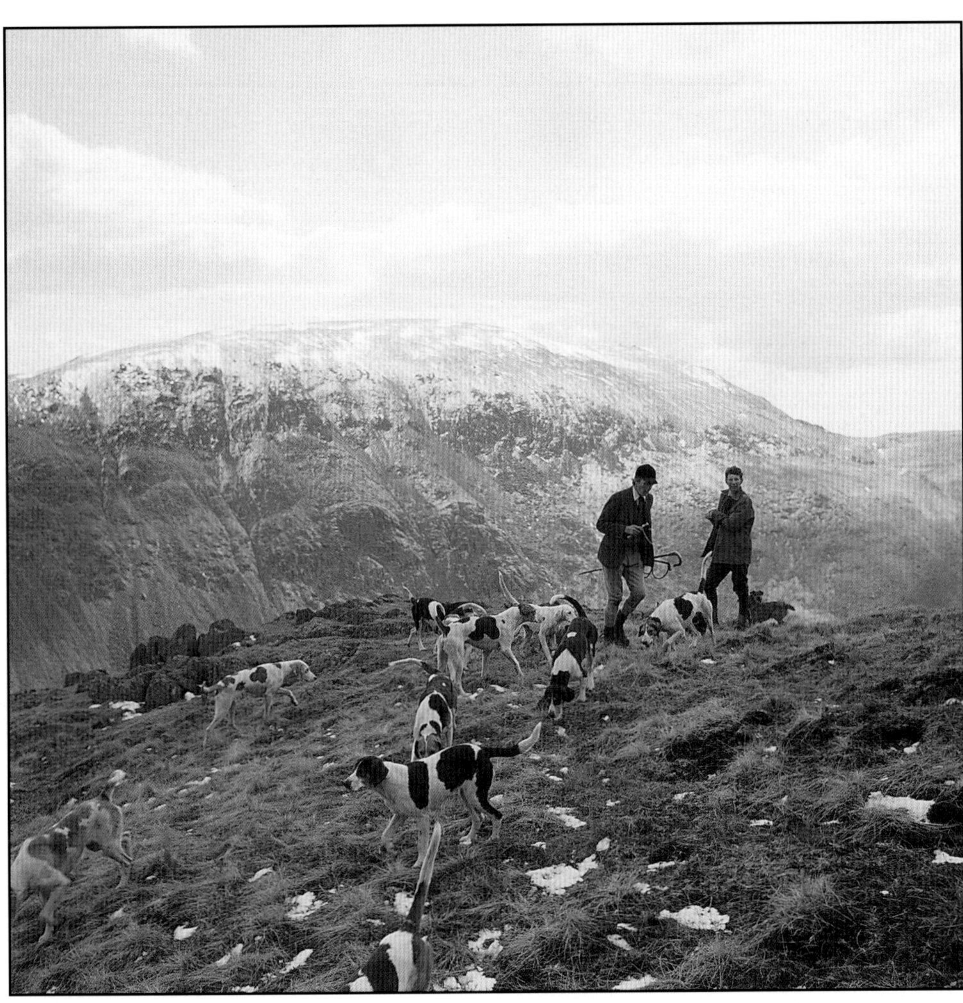

The Porter family have been masters of the Eskdale and Ennerdale Hunt since 1910. Edmund Porter, here with hounds high on the fells, has been huntsman since 1963 and master since 1979 in this rugged country.

The East ESSEX *Hunt*

It was raining heavily as East Essex huntsman John O'Shea fords a stream with his hounds, on their way to draw a covert.

What an attractive setting Panfield Hall makes for a lawn meet of the East Essex. Huntsman John O'Shea is flanked by joint masters Guy and Gill Lyster, whose retirement day this was.

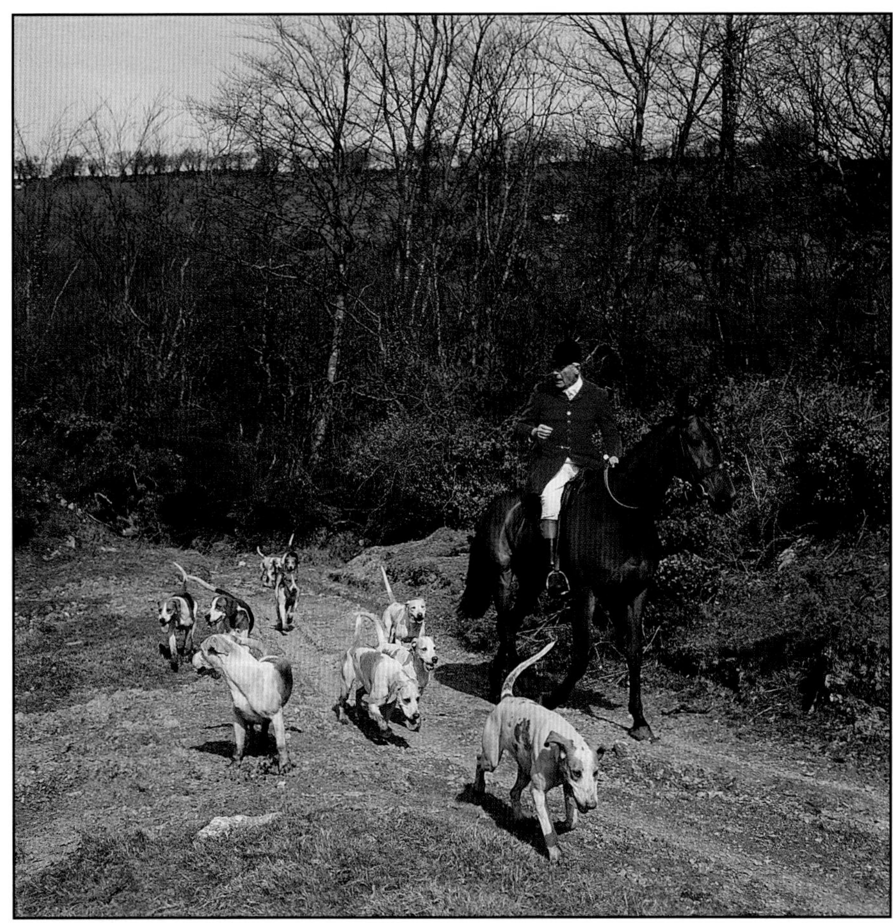

Jack Hosegood, who was MFH and huntsman from 1956-61 and 1964-80, bringing hounds out of a covert, past flowering gorse bushes.

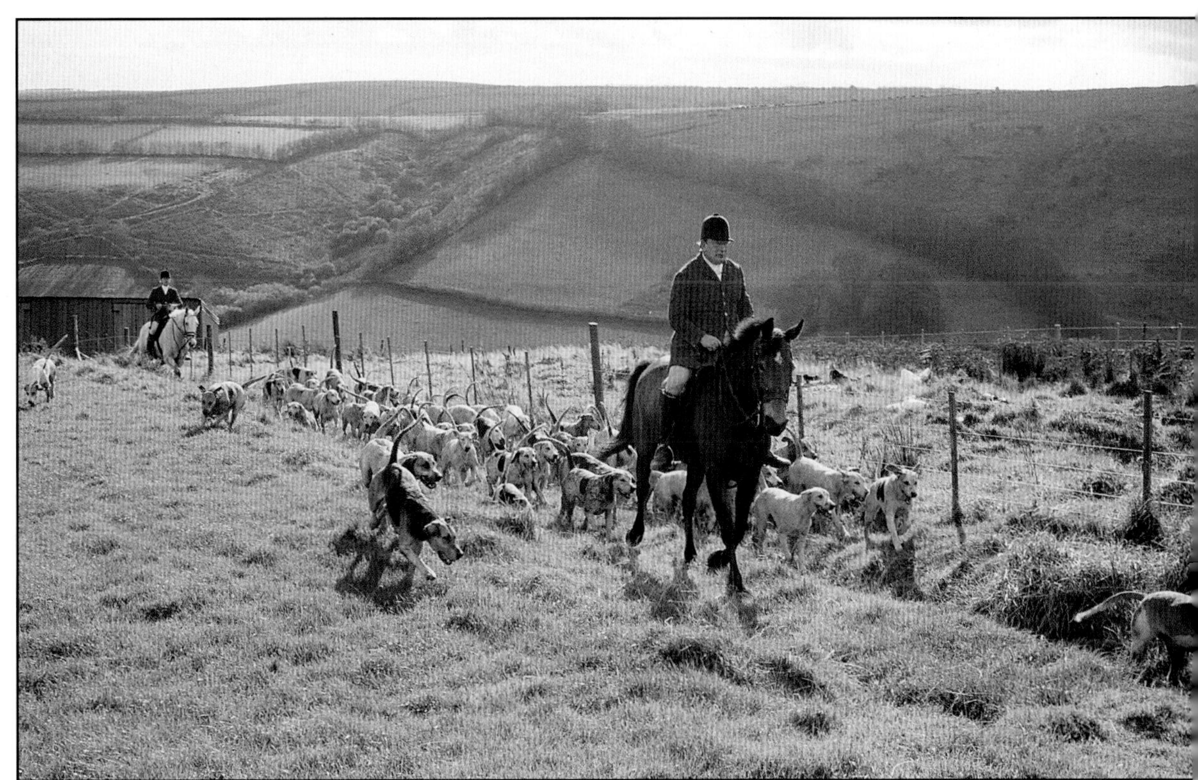

One of the all-time great masters and huntsmen, Capt Ronnie Wallace, with his hounds during a day's hunting on beautiful Exmoor. Capt Wallace was joint master and huntsman of the Heythrop from 1952-77, when he moved to the Exmoor Hunt, also known as 'The Stars of the West'.

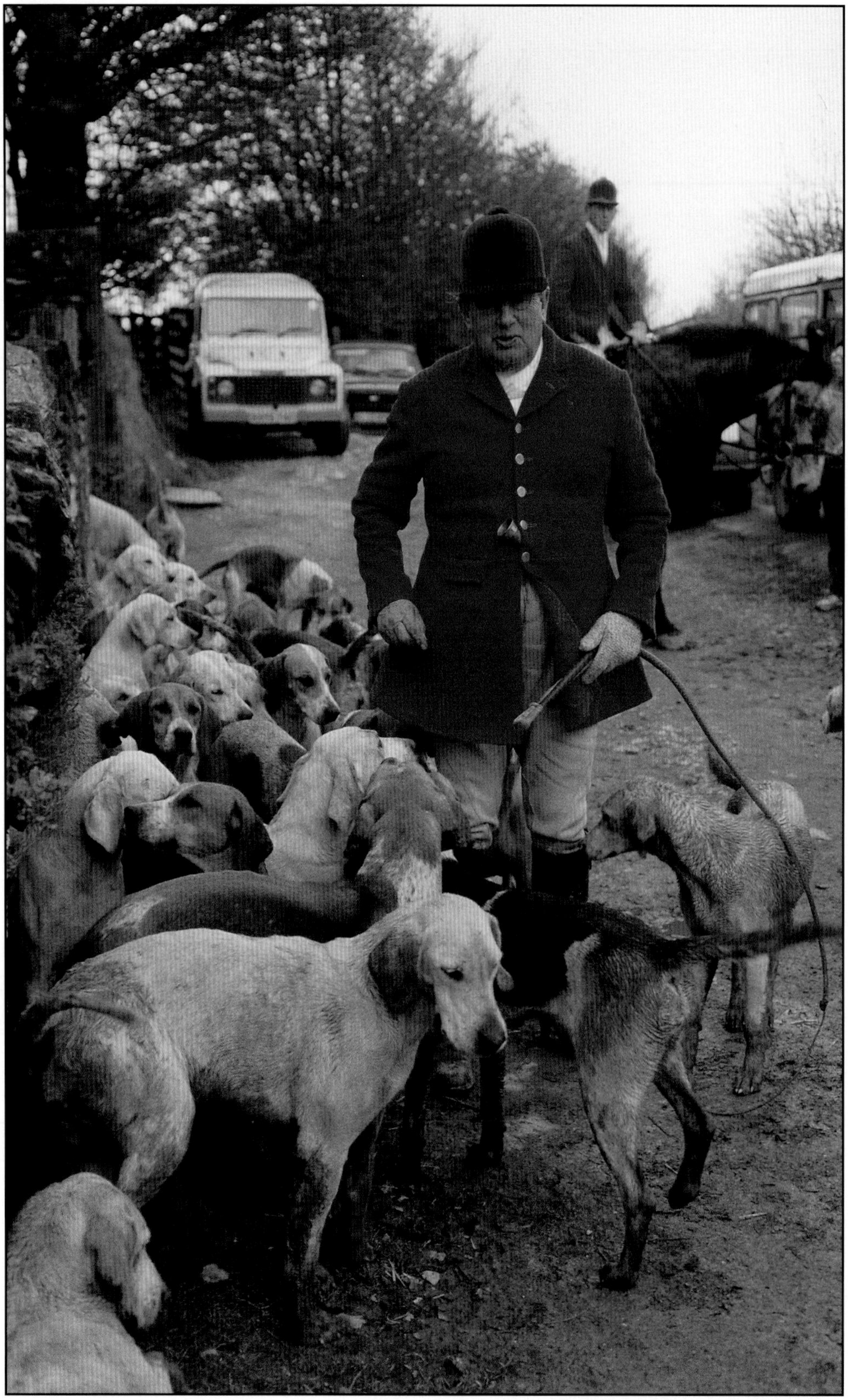

Capt Ronnie Wallace MFH with the muddy hounds at the end of a day which finished at Warren Farm.

FALLS

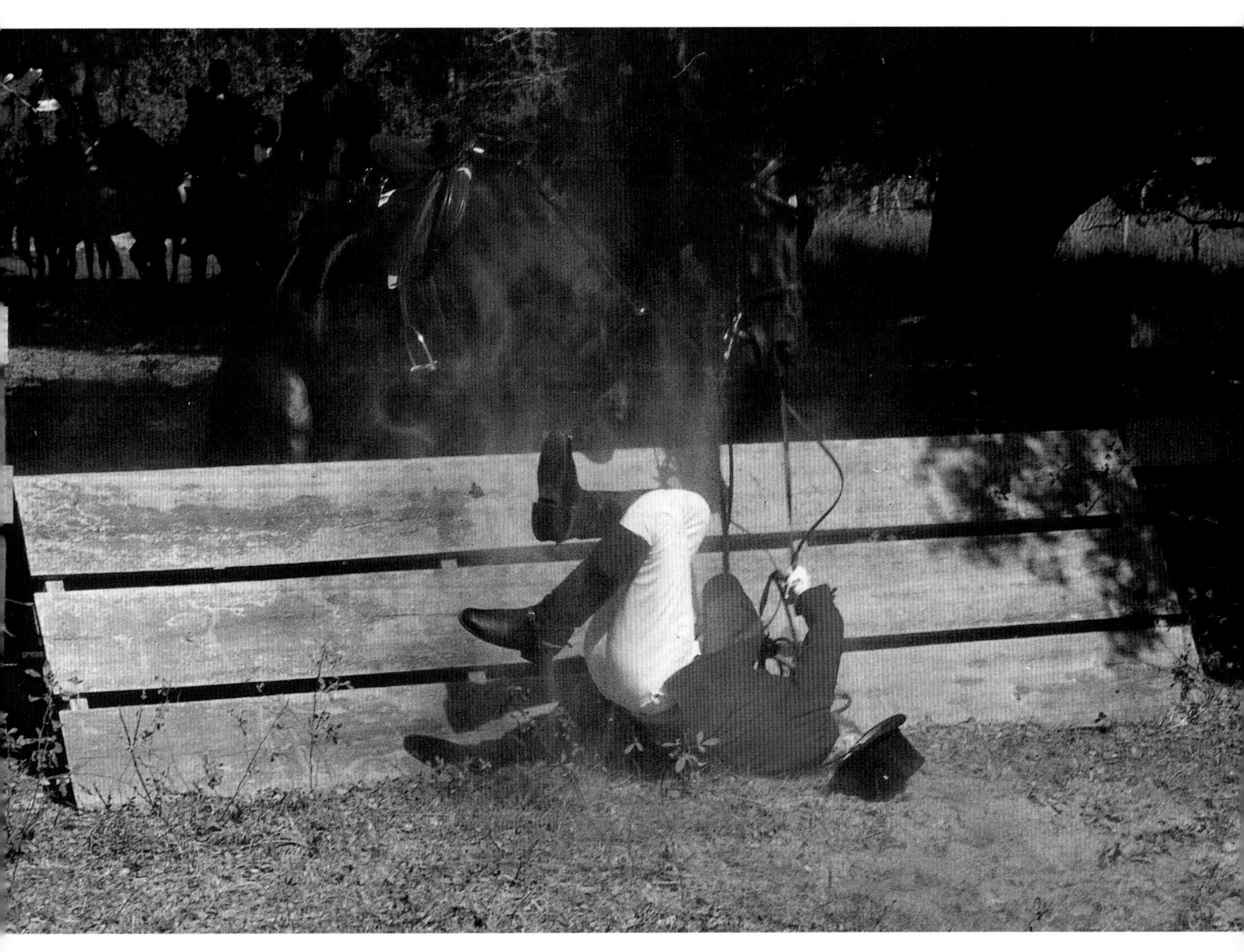

A Palm Beach faller, during a hunt in Florida, USA.

FALLS

A joint master of the Bicester with Whaddon Chase Hunt, in a rather unusual position!

"Well if I can clear the fence, why can't you?" A tricky situation with the Bicester with Whaddon Chase Hunt.

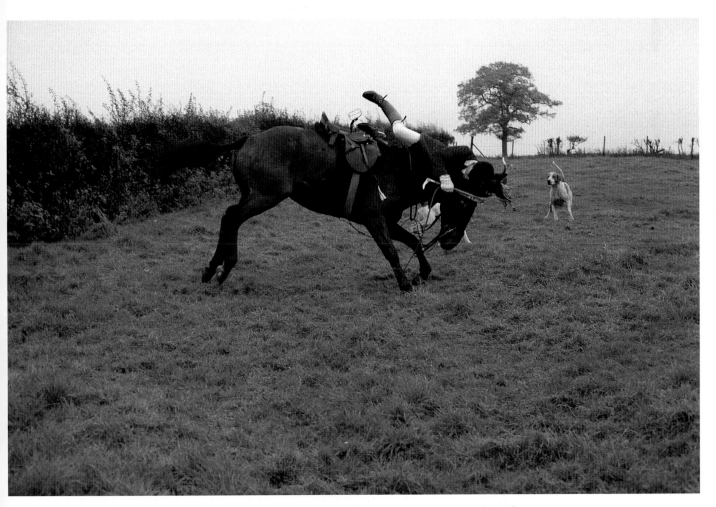

A Padua red Pytchley coat, about to collect some mud as the horse makes a bad mistake while jumping a style.

FALLS

This Meynell rider is in a very dangerous place, following a fall at a big thorn hedge.

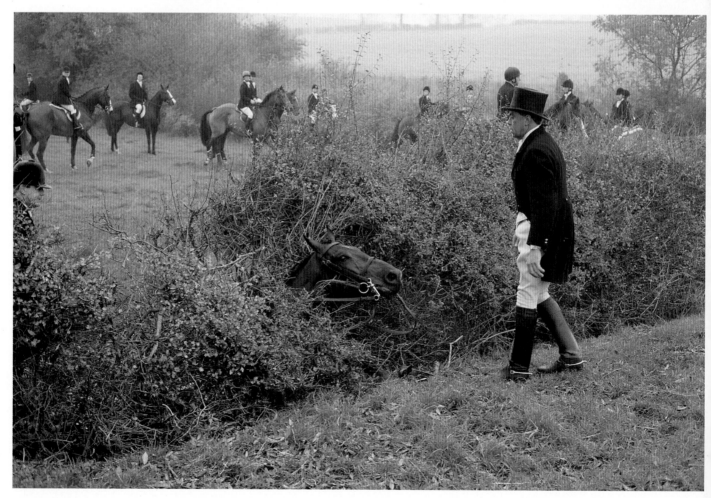

"Now what do I do?" asks this Quorn follower as his horse ends up in a deep ditch.

FAMILIES

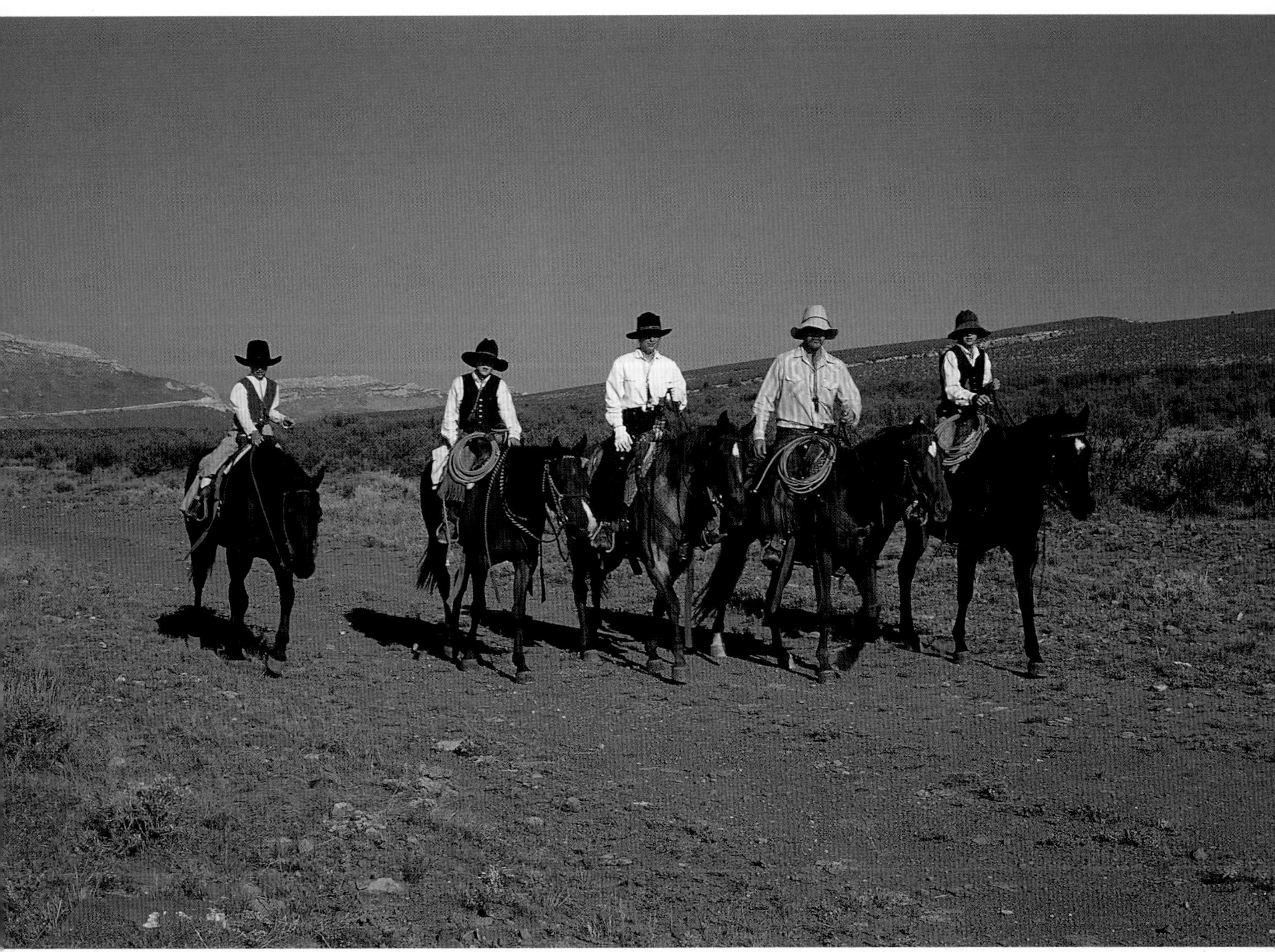

The Rosengreen family, Sam, Mary, Wesley, Shirl and Missi, who all help whip-in to Mr Jefford's hounds at Iron Mountain, Wyoming, USA.

F

FAMILIES

The Rowson family with the South Shropshire hounds. L to R: huntsman Michael Rowson, his wife Norma, daughter Diana, who is whipper-in to the Midland Hunt in Georgia USA, and her sister Clare.

The Barclay family celebrating 100 years as masters of the Puckeridge. Capt Charles Barclay MFH, surrounded by his children James, Diana, Ted and Robert, who have all been masters of foxhounds.

FAMILIES

The Dixey family. Emma Dixey, the first girl master of the Stowe beagles, with her grandfather Paul, hunt chairman of the Essex foxhounds and her father Charles, whose horse 'Castle Mane' won the 1999 Cheltenham foxhunter's steeplechase in great style.

One of the greatest families of hunt servants, the Maidens, have had members working with hunts since 1680. L to R: Jack Maiden - West Percy, Chris Maiden - Berkeley and Bert Maiden - Pytchley.

The FERNIE *Hunt* (LEICESTERSHIRE)

In his 31st and last season as huntsman to this well-known pack, Bruce Durno is seen taking his mostly tricoloured hounds to draw, on one of his final days carrying the horn.

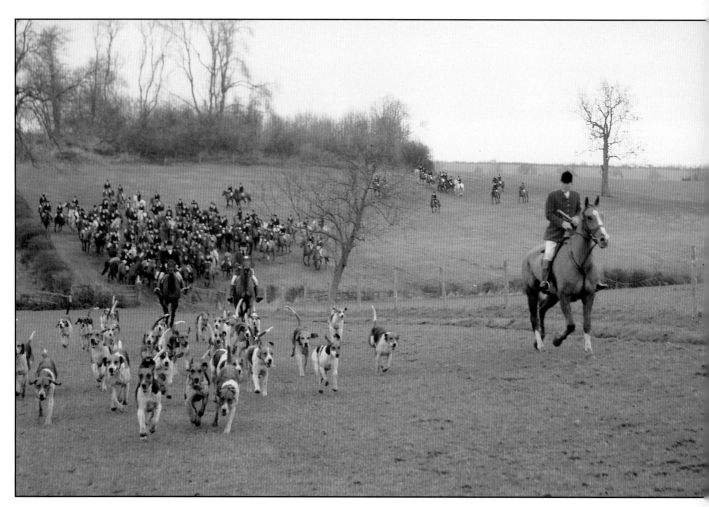

Bruce Durno, who hunted the Fernie from 1966-97, leading hounds and a big field across country on the way to draw a covert.

The FIFE *Hunt* (SCOTLAND)

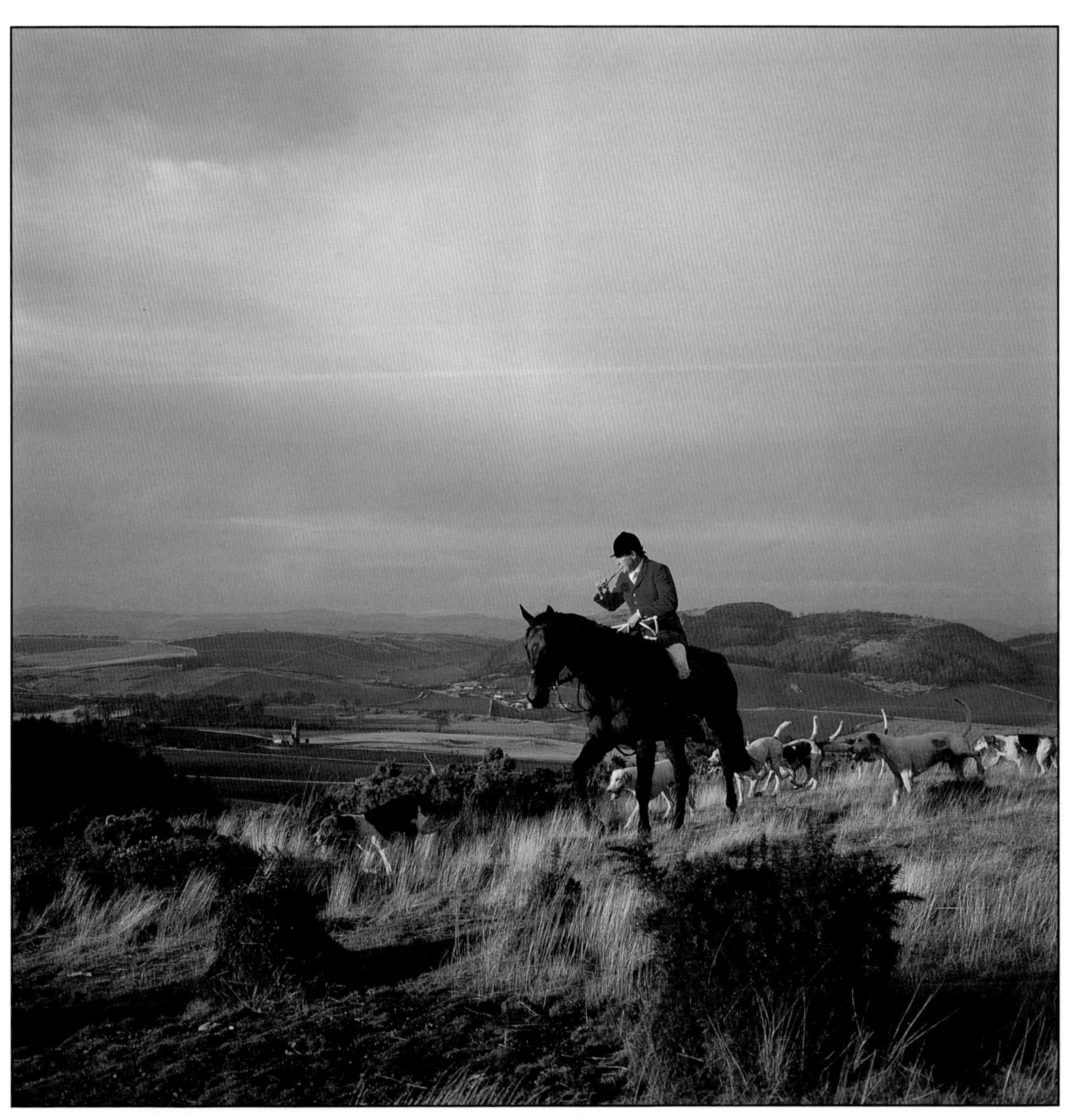

John Gilmour who has been a master of the Fife Hunt since 1973, casting hounds during a good hunt on high ground above Dunbog as late afternoon sunshine lights up the scene. This was in December 1986, during the Fife Hunt's bi-centenary season.

The FLINT AND DENBIGH *Hunt* (NORTH WALES)

With a rocky escarpment towering behind, huntsman Geoff Sales is pictured with hounds and a group of young riders from a well attended pony club camp, close to the kennels.

The Flint and Denbigh, with their joint master and huntsman Sir Watkin Williams-Wynn, in open country in North Wales. Sir Watkin was also a master of his family pack, the Wynnstay, which hounds he owns.

FOG

Joint master and huntsman to the Eryri hounds, Richard Williams, blowing "gone to ground", as the pack mark in a terribly rocky place, on the foothills of Snowdon and in the fog.

Lady Melissa Brooke, joint master of the County Limerick Hunt, discussing the prospects of the fog lifting with her huntsman Hugh Robards.

FOG

Spanish moss hanging from Live Oak trees, as the field of the South Creek foxhounds enjoy a hunt in the fog near Tampa, Florida, USA.

Pytchley huntsman Peter Jones leading his hounds and a large Saturday field through the fog in search of clearer conditions.

Hard pushed by the North Herefordshire hounds, this fox runs through a farmyard in an effort to throw the pack off his scent.

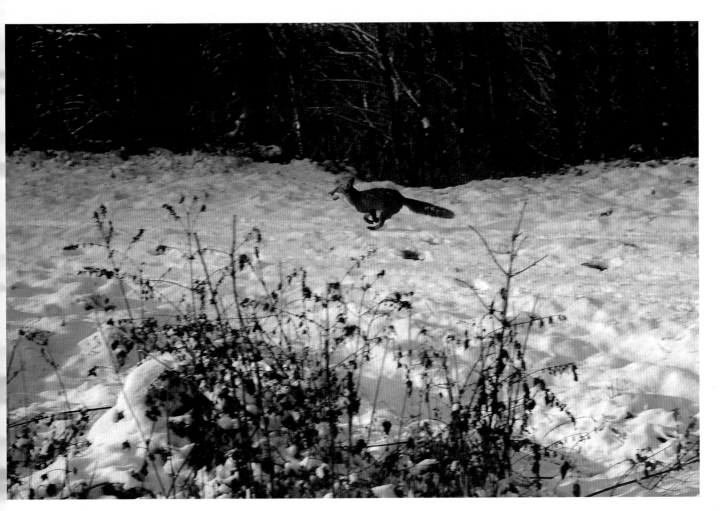

A Warwickshire fox making good speed across a snowy landscape.

The GALWAY BLAZERS *Hunt* (IRELAND)

A joint master of the Galway Blazers Hunt from 1983-97, Tom Moore, clears a typical Galway stone wall in good style.

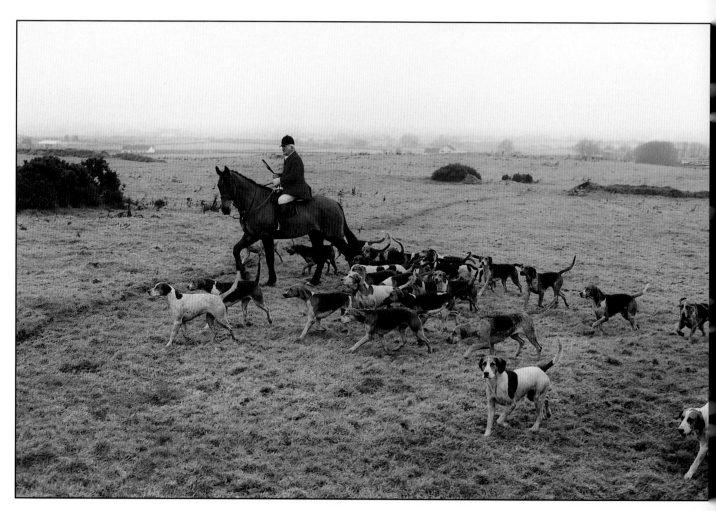

Michael Dempsey, for so many years joint master and huntsman to the Galway Blazers Hunt, taking hounds to draw near Loughrea on a 'soft' day.

GATES

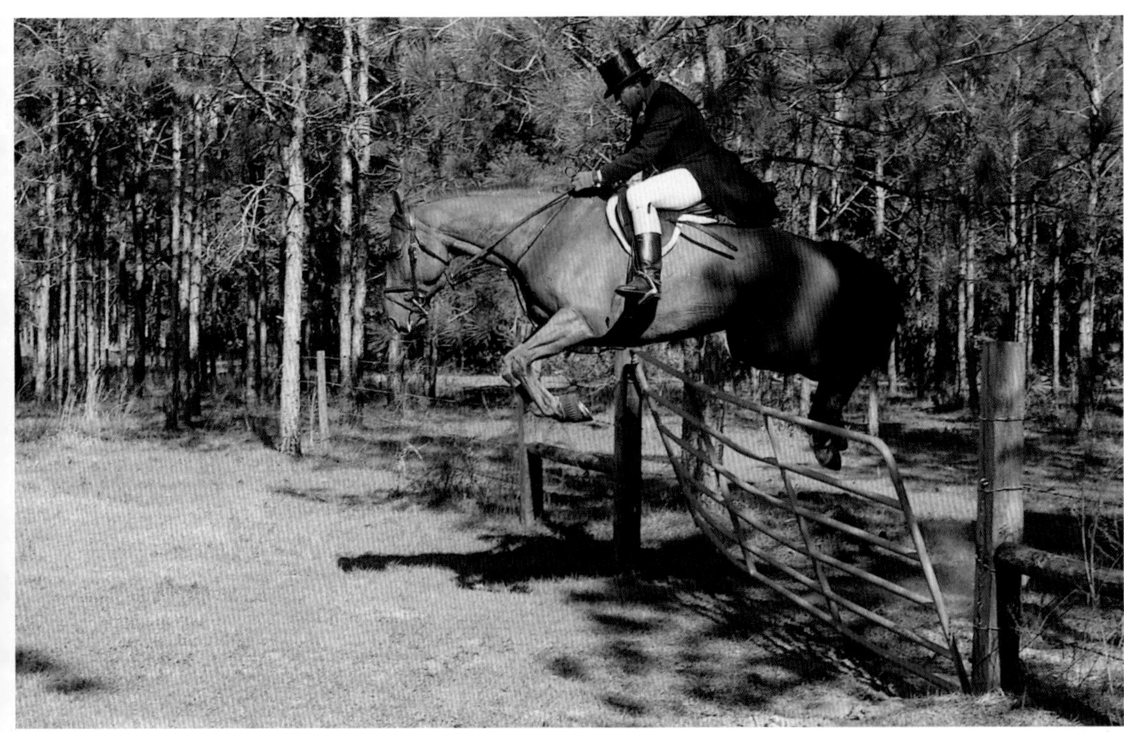

Irish visitor Aidan O'Connell jumping a big iron gate during the All Florida meet, near Tampa, USA.

A five barred wooden gate poses no problems for Michael Bletsoe-Brown MFH Pytchley Hunt.

G

The
GLAMORGAN
Hunt
(SOUTH WALES)

Huntsman Neil Burton taking hounds to draw along a green, leafy avenue of trees. This was from the opening meet, held at St. Mary Church on 19 October – hence the very summer-like foliage.

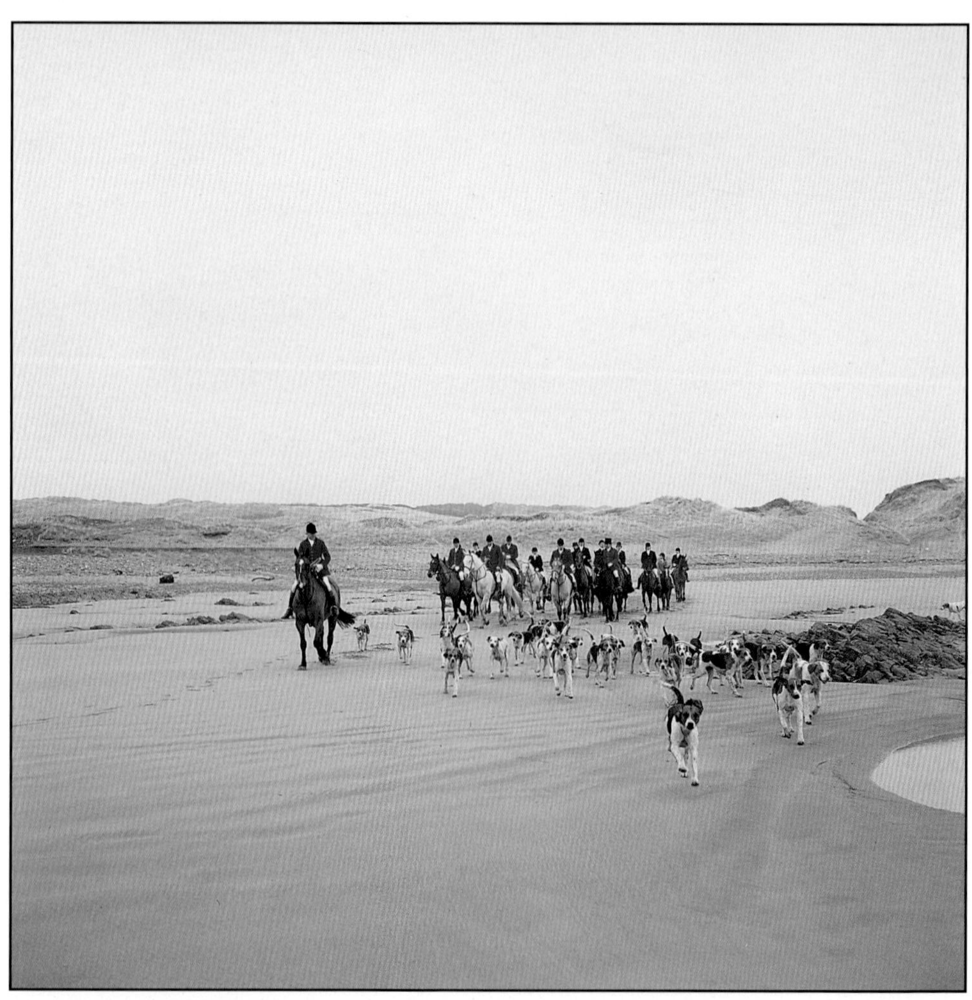

A most unusual setting for the Glamorgan Hunt as the day ends on sand dunes and the beach, on the coast of South Wales.

The GOLDEN VALLEY *Hunt* (WELSH BORDERS)

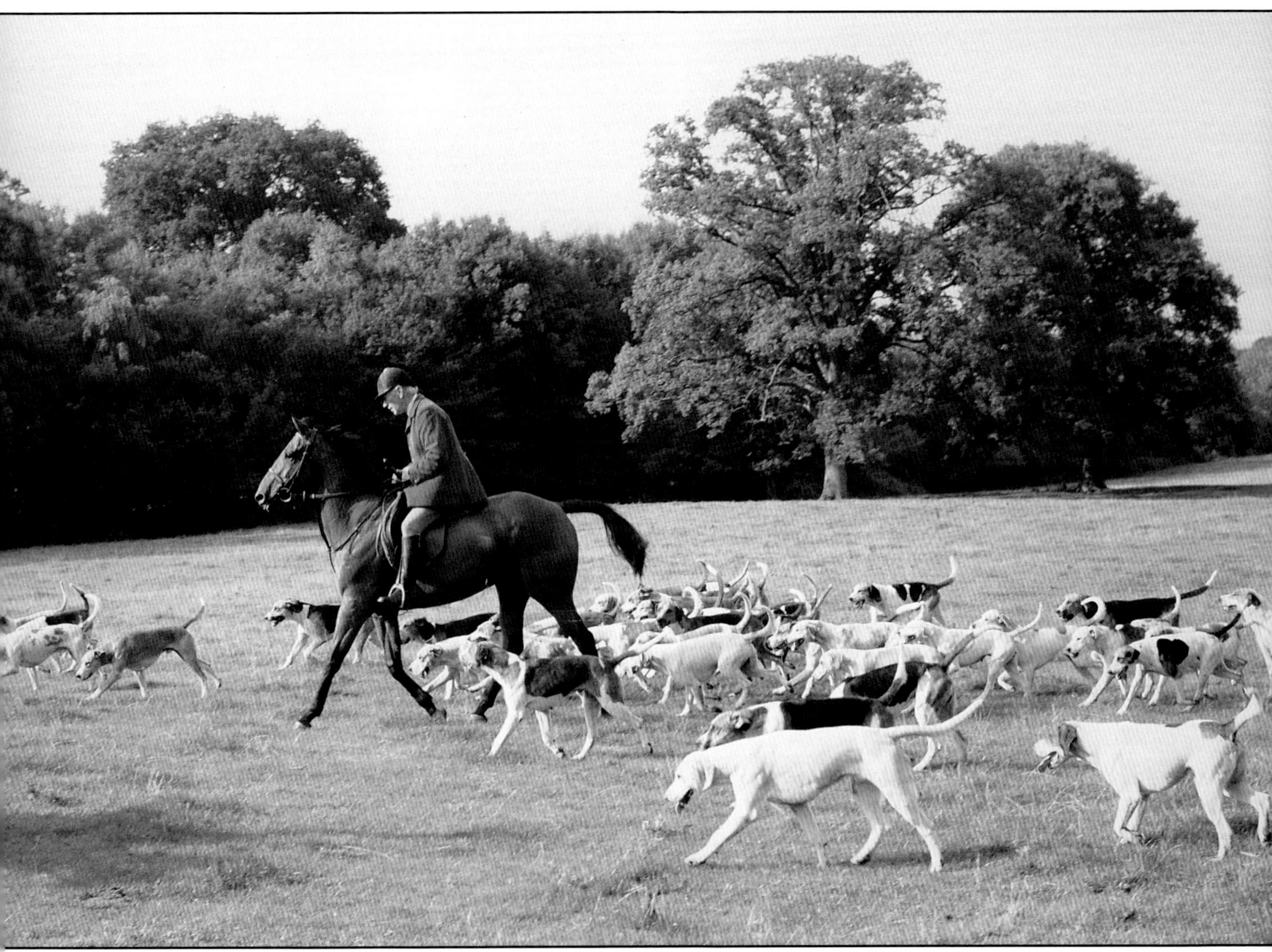

Longest serving master of foxhounds with the same pack in the United Kingdom, Vivian Bishop, has been with the Golden Valley, which he helped to form, since 1945. For much of this time he hunted hounds, often riding top class point-to-point horses or hunter chasers.

G

The
GREEN CREEK
Hunt
(UNITED STATES OF AMERICA)

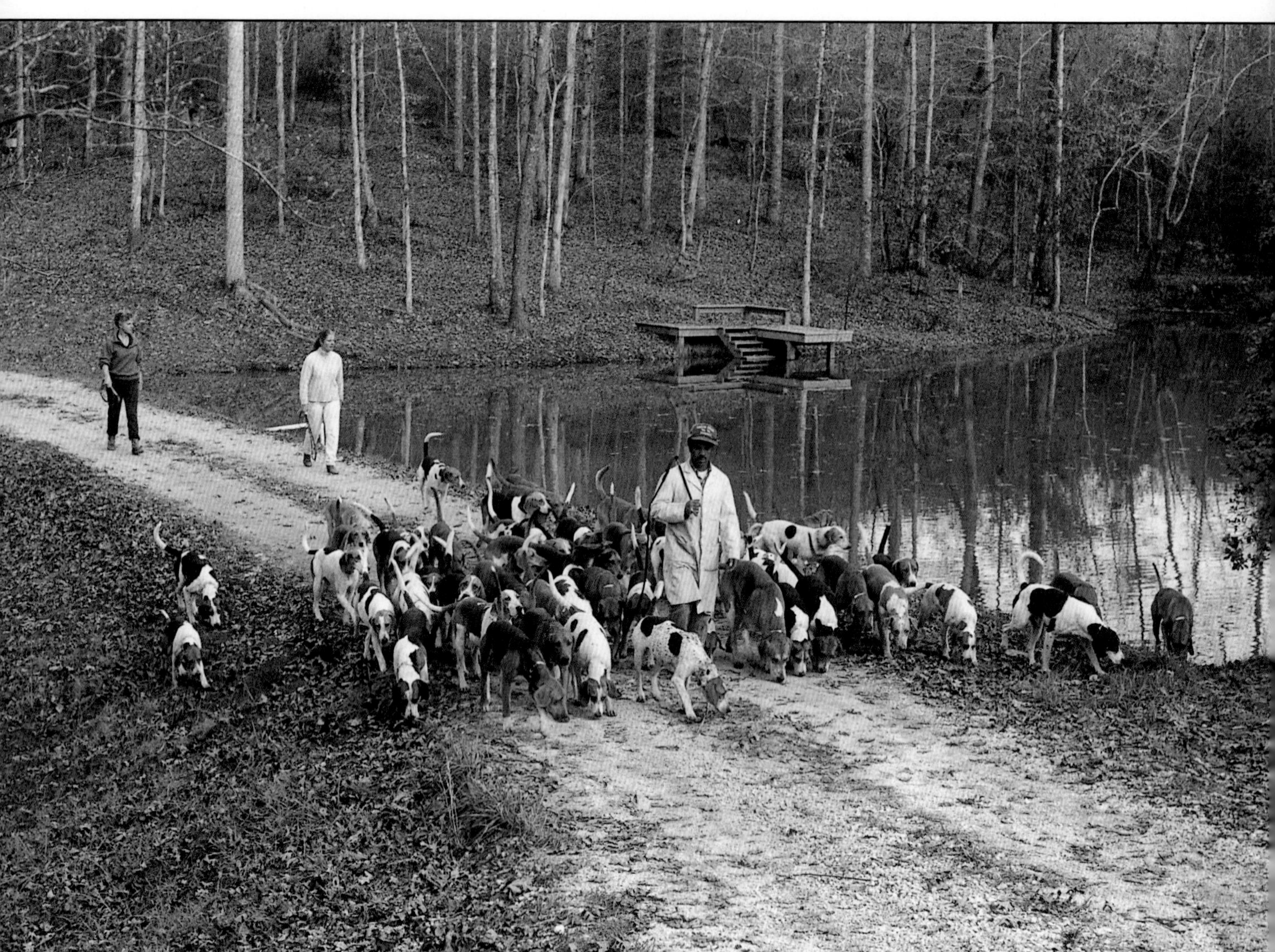

Jefferson 'Tot' Goodwin, joint master and huntsman to the Green Creek Hunt, walking hounds out from the kennels in North Carolina, USA.

The GREEN SPRING VALLEY *Hunt* (UNITED STATES OF AMERICA)

The Green Spring Valley hounds in Maryland, with their huntsman Andrew Barclay, pause by the beautiful hunt club house while walking out from the kennels on exercise.

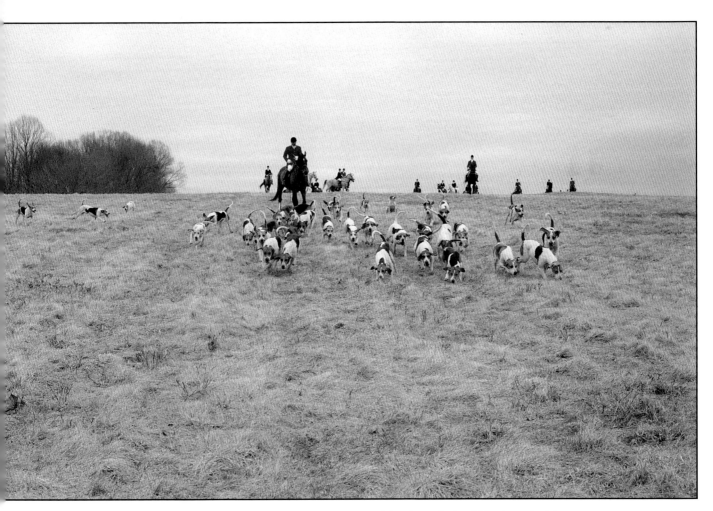

Huntsman Andrew Barclay makes a good cast, and the Green Spring Valley hounds pick up the scent again as the mounted field appear on the skyline.

G

The
GREENVILLE COUNTY
Hunt

(UNITED STATES OF AMERICA)

With the Glassy Mountain as a backdrop, joint master and huntsman Gerald Pack leads the Greenville County Hunt across country during autumn hunting in North Carolina, USA.

The HAMILTON *Hunt* (CANADA)

Hank Martin, joint master of the Hamilton Hunt, jumping a coop with hunt secretary Kathy Ellis in the colourful fall, in Canada.

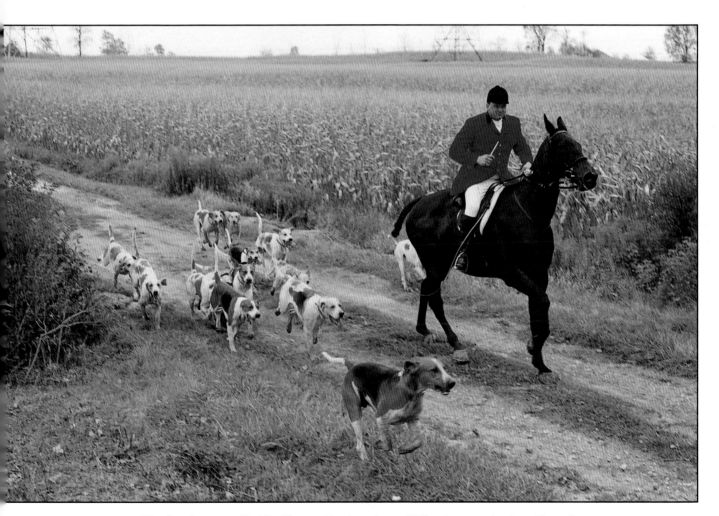

Hamilton huntsman Paul Luckhurst taking hounds to a Holloa, in a area dominated by maize fields.

The HAMPSHIRE *Hunt*

Huntsman Bob Collins conjures a huge jump out of his useful hunter, to clear a wide thorn hedge. Note the field on the hillside behind.

HEDGES

This good hedge is still green as John Whitehouse, MH Ross Harriers, soars over.

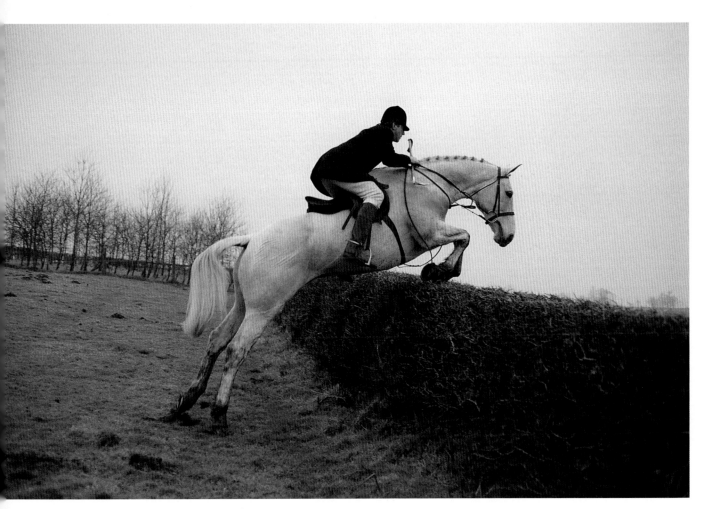

The Hon Johnny Greenall, MFH Meynell Hunt, attacking a tall, wide thorn hedge during a good hunt in the afternoon.

H

HEDGES

A very wide hedge being jumped in good style by Greg Mousley, MH Dove Valley mink hounds.

Portman joint master Percy Tory in action during a good hunt in the rain.

The North HEREFORDSHIRE *Hunt*

A big field on the move across a grassy hillside. In the centre are the three joint masters, Ian Haynes, Xenia Folkes and Alan Bassett.

After years of hoping, I was finally able to take this picture of huntsman Harley Godsall leading the North Herefordshire hounds from a meet at Hampton Court, the home of joint master Xenia Folkes and her husband James.

H

The

HEYTHROP

Hunt

(OXFORDSHIRE AND GLOUCESTERSHIRE)

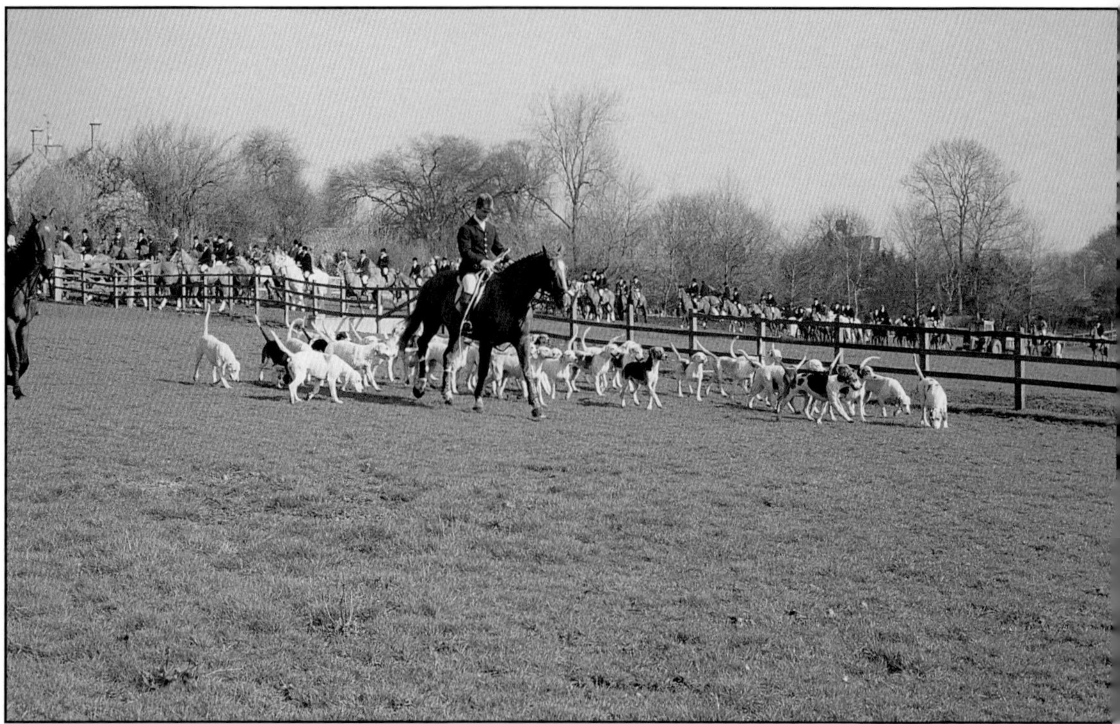

Huntsman Anthony Adams leading hounds and a huge field from their Cheltenham Wednesday meet, near Bourton on the Water.

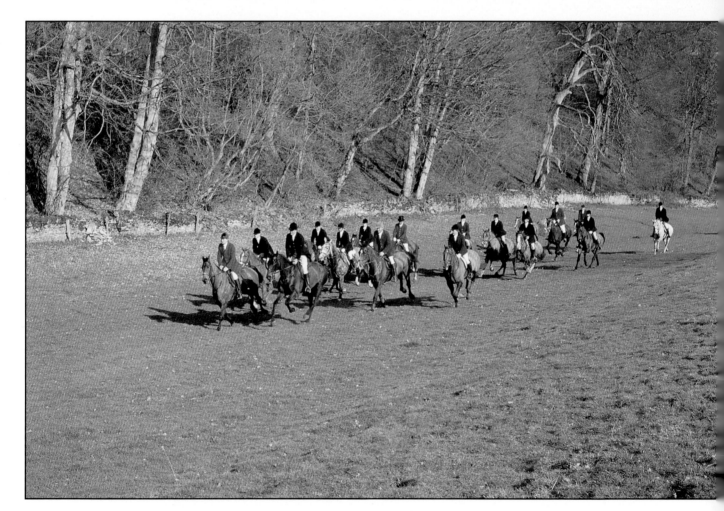

Joint Hon. Sec. Guy Avis heading the field along a typical, pretty, Cotswold valley. The masters and hunt staff wear green coats, indicating that the Heythrop country was hunted by the Duke of Beaufort until 1835.

The HIGH PEAK HARRIERS (DERBYSHIRE)

The High Peak harriers in full cry in their lovely stone wall country, in Derbyshire.

HOUND SHOWS

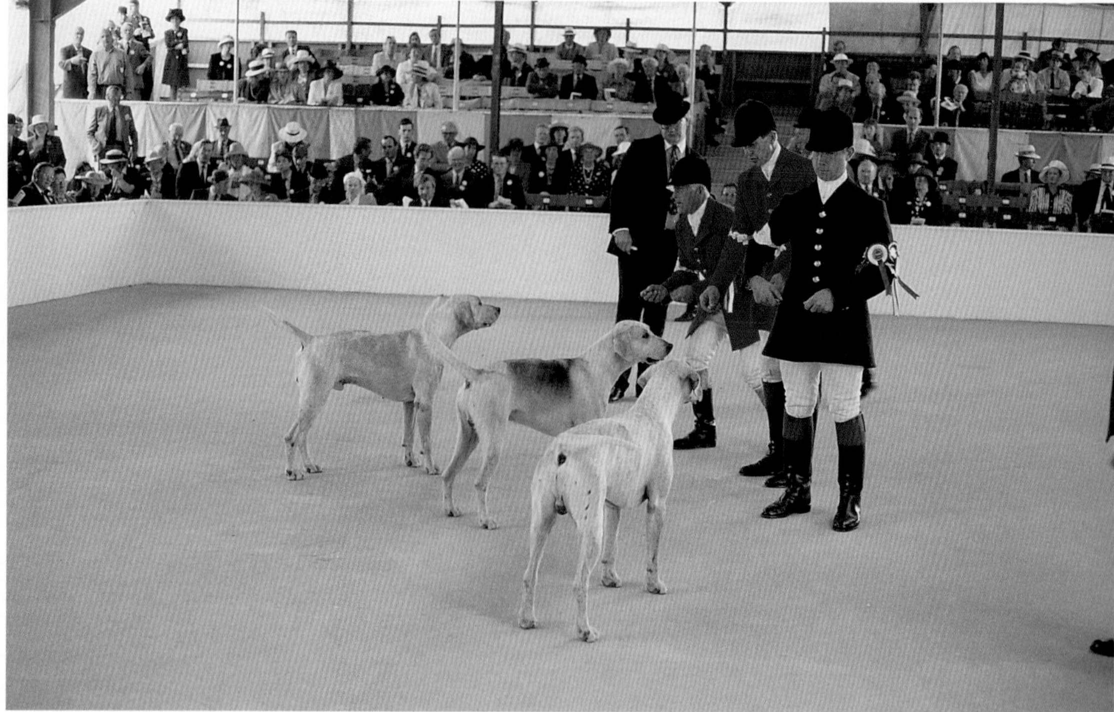

Showing hounds in the Doghound championship at Peterborough are Michael Rowson (South Shropshire), Tony Wright (Exmoor) and Anthony Adams (Heythrop).

Peterborough champion bitch, North Cotswold 'Grapefruit', shown by Charlie White and admired by walkers Mr and Mrs Charlie Warren and the joint masters Sophia and Nigel Peel.

HOUND SHOWS

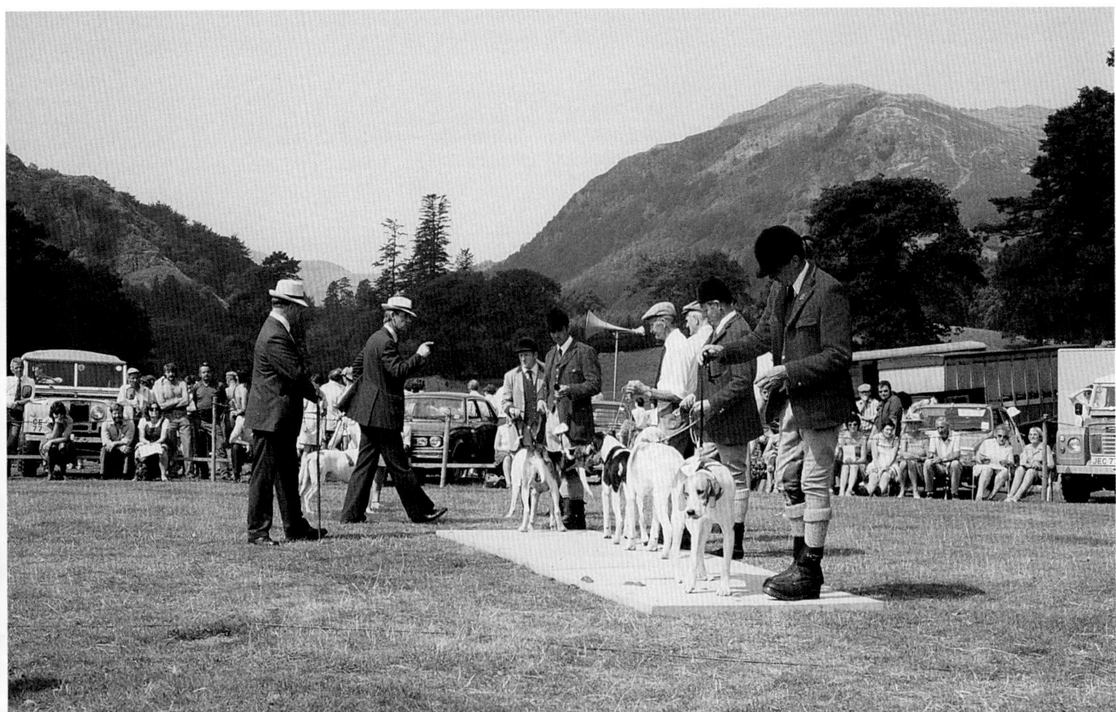

A spectacular setting, beneath towering fells, as a class is judged at Rydal fell foxhound show in the Lake District of north-west England.

Judging in progress at Lowther to find the champion foxhound. Showing hounds are Barry Todhunter (Blencathra) and Andrew Proe (College Valley).

H

HOUND SHOWS

Michael Kennedy (Kilmoganny) and Nigel Cox (Waterford) running hounds in the bitch championship at the Irish foxhound show.

With the trophies won by South Shropshire 'Chorus' at Honiton (shown by Michael Rowson and held by whipper-in Richard Evans) is hunt chairman Lindsay Wallace, flanked by joint masters Andrew Cook and Anne Stevens.

HOUND SHOWS

Brecon and Talybont huntsman Ian Hawkins showing his champion bitch 'Sonic', at the Welsh foxhound show held at Builth Wells.

Supreme champion foxhound at the Virginia show, Midland 'Import', shown by huntsman Mark Dixon and admired by Mason Lampton MFH, Martin Scott (judge), Ben Hardaway MFH and Leander McMillen MFH (judge).

A white frost is an unusual sight in Alabama so a warming bonfire was lit to warm participants and spectators before the action began.

With numbered hounds at a Moccasin Gap meet are L to R: John Lowery MFH (Full Cry); Mark Powell (Iroquois kennel huntsman); Betsy Park (Millbrook huntsman); Allen Forney (Howard County-Iron Bridge huntsman); Jerry Miller MFH (Iroquois); Mason Lampton MFH (Midland); Randy Waterman MFH (Piedmont); Epp Wilson MFH (Belle Meade).

HOUND TRIALS

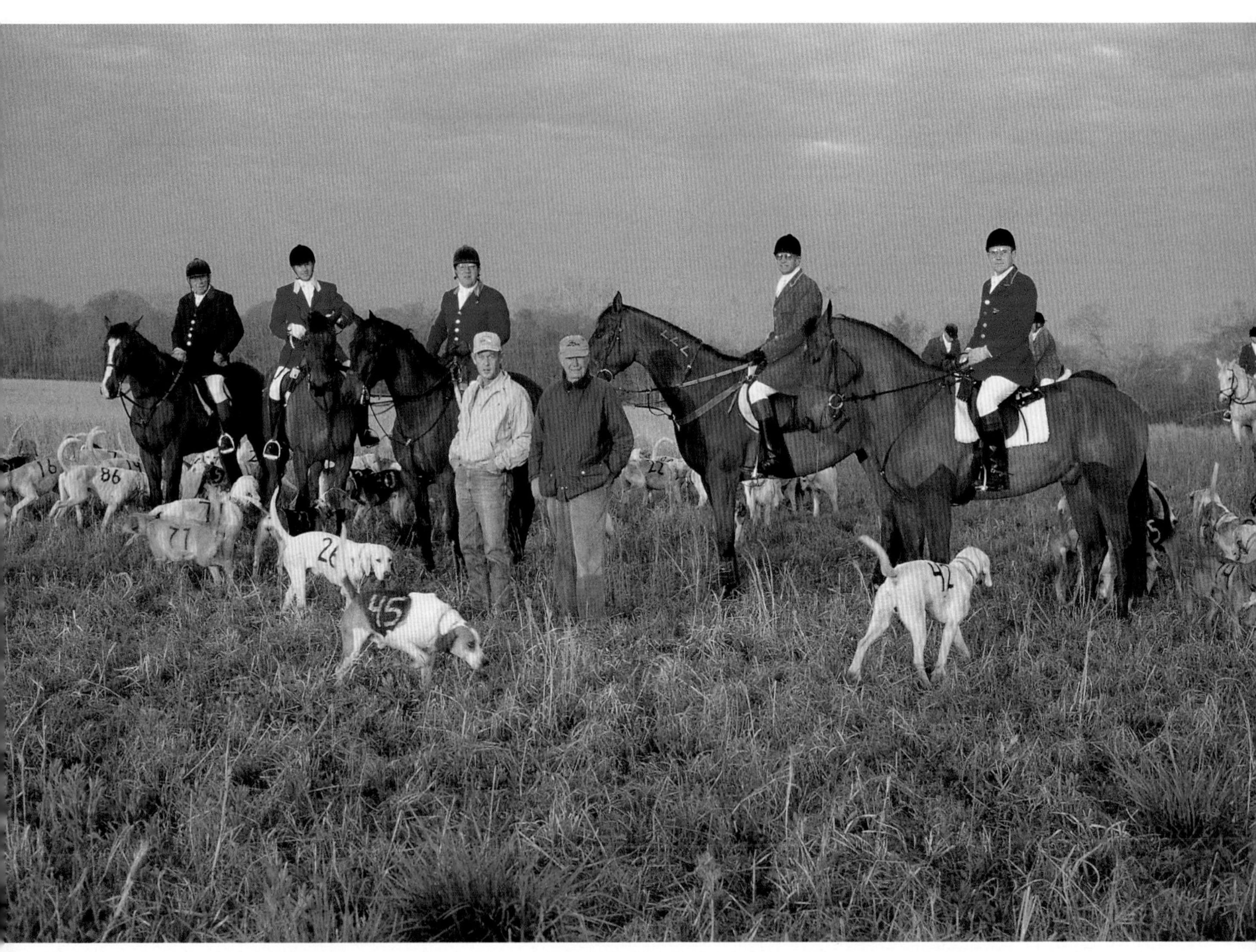

With numbered hounds at the meet are, L to R, John Lowery MFH (Full Cry), Epp Wilson MFH (Belle Meade), Mason Lampton MFH (Midland), Tommy Coleman MFH (Whitworth) and Charles Hughes MFH (Whitworth). On foot are Ben Hardaway III MFH (Midland) and host Frank Rutland.

Five local riders who enjoyed the hunt, riding western style.

The big field on the move on a misty morning in the swamps of Alabama.

HUNT BREAKFASTS

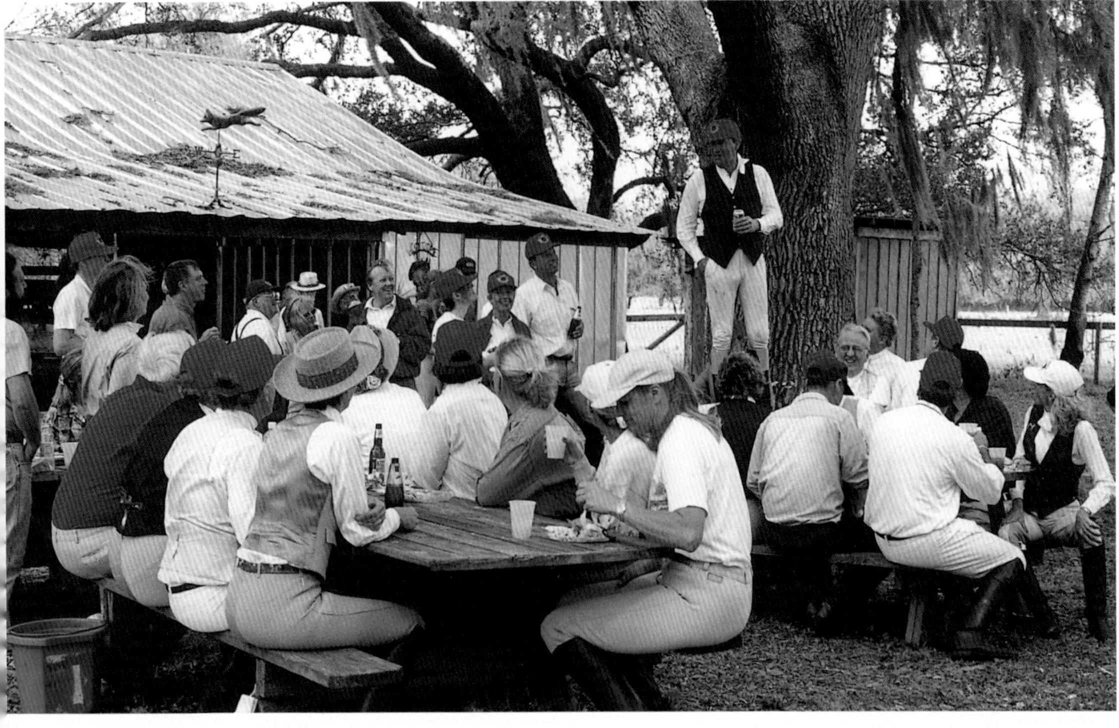

A splendid hunt breakfast at the end of the All Florida meet, near Tampa, USA, when around 100 riders followed hounds.

Chicken in the basket and drinks round a blazing log fire, at the end of a day with the Midland hounds in Georgia USA.

H

The HYDE PARK RALLY

Leading the way from the start in Machynlleth are Richard Williams MFH (Eryri) and David Davies huntsman David Jones.

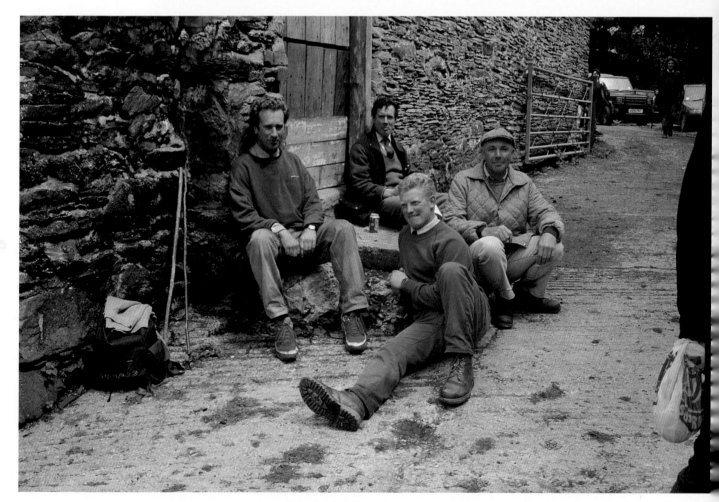

Lunch break for aching legs! L to R: Adrian Dangar MFH (Sinnington), Sam Butler MFH (Warwickshire), Andrew Cook MFH (South Shropshire) and Jim McIvor, terrier man to the United pack.

Halfway to London and the Welsh marchers pour down a grassy hillside in great spirits.

An unforgettable sight, looking out over the huge crowds from the stage in Hyde Park on 10 July 1997.

I

The
IROQUOIS
Hunt
(UNITED STATES OF AMERICA)

The Bishop of Lexington, blessing the Iroquois hounds, in a ceremony at the hunt kennels on the day of the opening meet. In the centre is joint master and huntsman Jerry Miller.

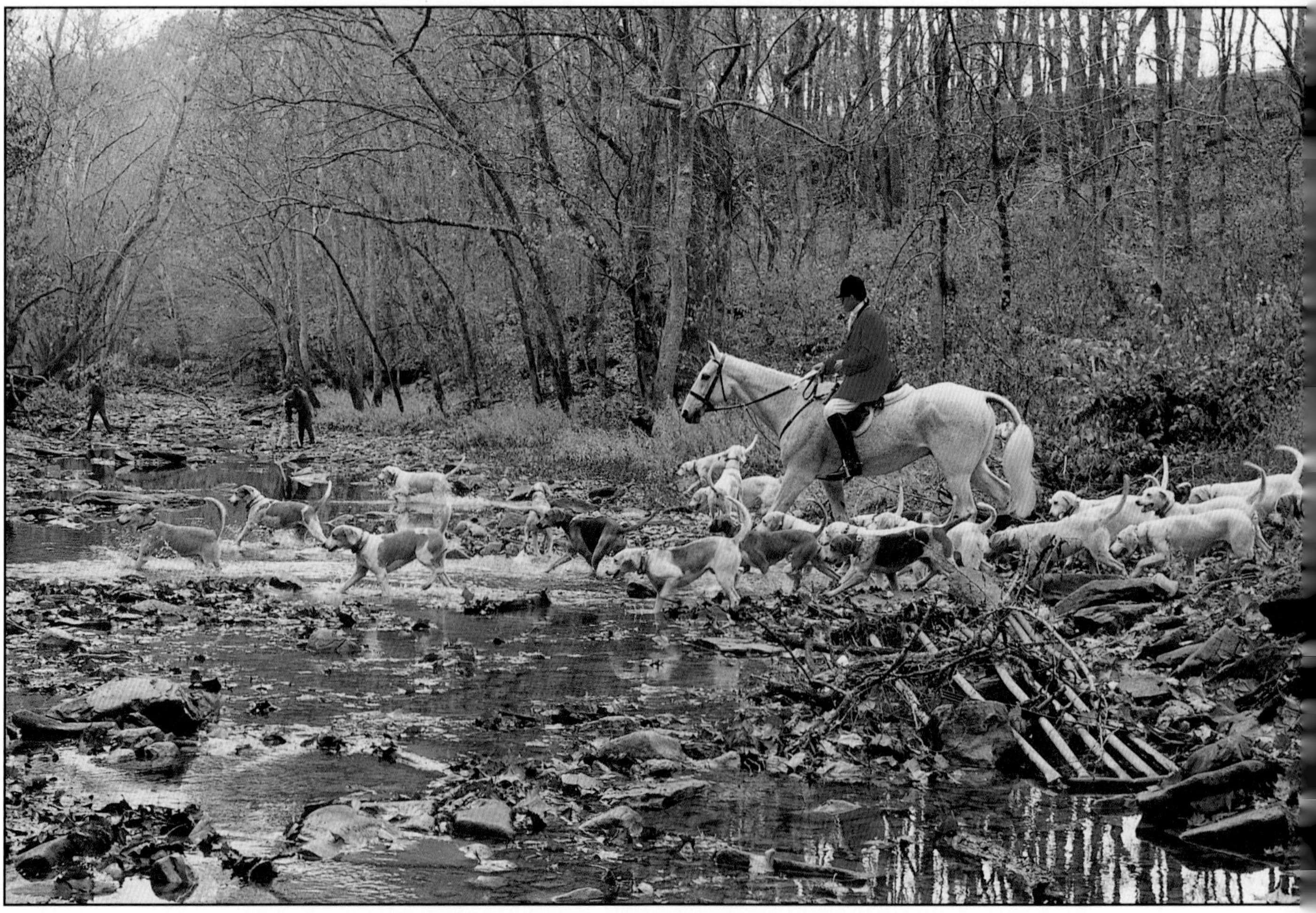

With the trees almost bare of leaves, joint master and huntsman Jerry Miller leads the Iroquois hounds across a creek, on the way to draw.

The ISLE OF WIGHT FOOT BEAGLES

Staff and masters at the hunt's 90th birthday meet at Little East Standen, the same venue as their first meet in 1907.

The Isle of Wight foot beagles, headed by the huntsman Paul Whittington, walking home at the end of a day held to celebrate the packs 90th birthday, in January 1997.

Mr JEFFORD'S *Hunt* (UNITED STATES OF AMERICA)

Mr Jefford's hunt staff, at Iron Mountain in Wyoming, wearing their summer uniform. Sue Blackmore whipper-in; huntsman Martyn Blackmore and whipper-in Jack Hettinger.

With the foot hills of the Rockies in the distance and some 7,000 feet above sea level, huntsman Martyn Blackmore leads Mr Jefford's black-and-tan Penn-Mary-Del hounds across a prairie-like country in Wyoming, on a day when the temperature reached 90 degrees Fahrenheit.

The KILKENNY *Hunt* (IRELAND)

Major Victor McCalmont, MFH from 1949-1993, taking hounds to draw across lovely old Irish turf. For much of his mastership 'The Major' carried the horn producing great sport. He also bred 'Famous', champion at Peterborough Royal Foxhound Show in 1978.

Kilkenny huntsman Paddy McDonald putting hounds in to draw a covert on a very wet morning.

Bedale joint master and huntsman Peter Hill-Walker, with hounds after catching a fox at the end of a useful hunt.

Adrian Dangar, joint master and huntsman of the Sinnington, with hounds after they had brought a good hunt to a successful conclusion at dusk.

The KILMOGANNY *Hunt* (IRELAND)

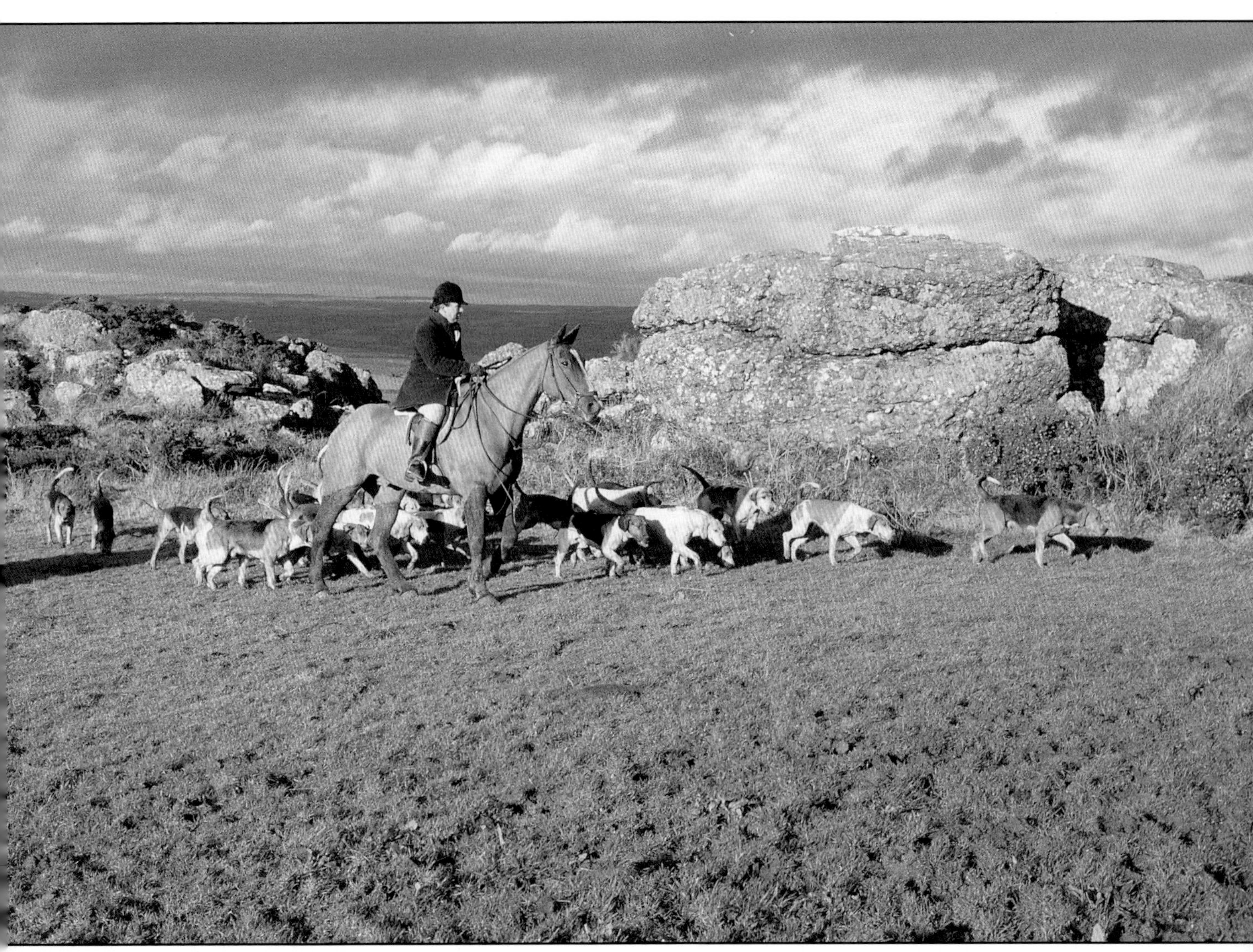

Rory Dicker, joint master and huntsman of the Kilmoganny, with hounds drawing over a rocky landscape in Ireland. The hunt staff wear green coats because, until 1987, the Kilmoganny was a harrier pack.

K

The
KYRE BLOODHOUNDS

The Kyre bloodhounds, led by their senior master and huntsman Edward Hammond, hacking home at last light after an excellent day from Grafton Farm, Pudleston, Herefordshire.

The LEDBURY *Hunt* (HEREFORDSHIRE, WORCESTERSHIRE & GLOUCESTERSHIRE)

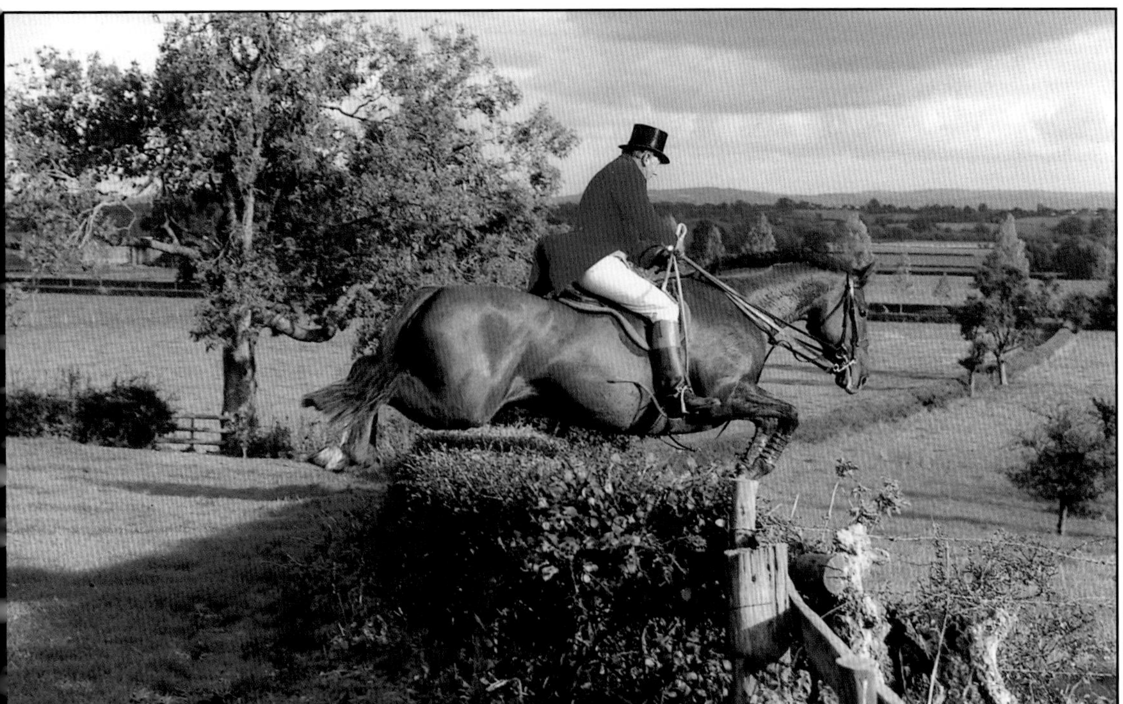

Elegantly attired top show rider and one time master of the Ledbury, Robert Oliver, takes a good thorn hedge, with drop, in fine style after the opening meet.

The Ledbury Hunt, with the Malvern Hills in the background, moving across splendid old turf during their opening meet day, from Corse Lawn.

L

The
LIVE OAK
Hunt
(UNITED STATES OF AMERICA)

Marty and Daphne Wood, joint masters of the Live Oak hounds, presenting Jim Meads with champagne, as their hunt was the 400th different one he had photographed.

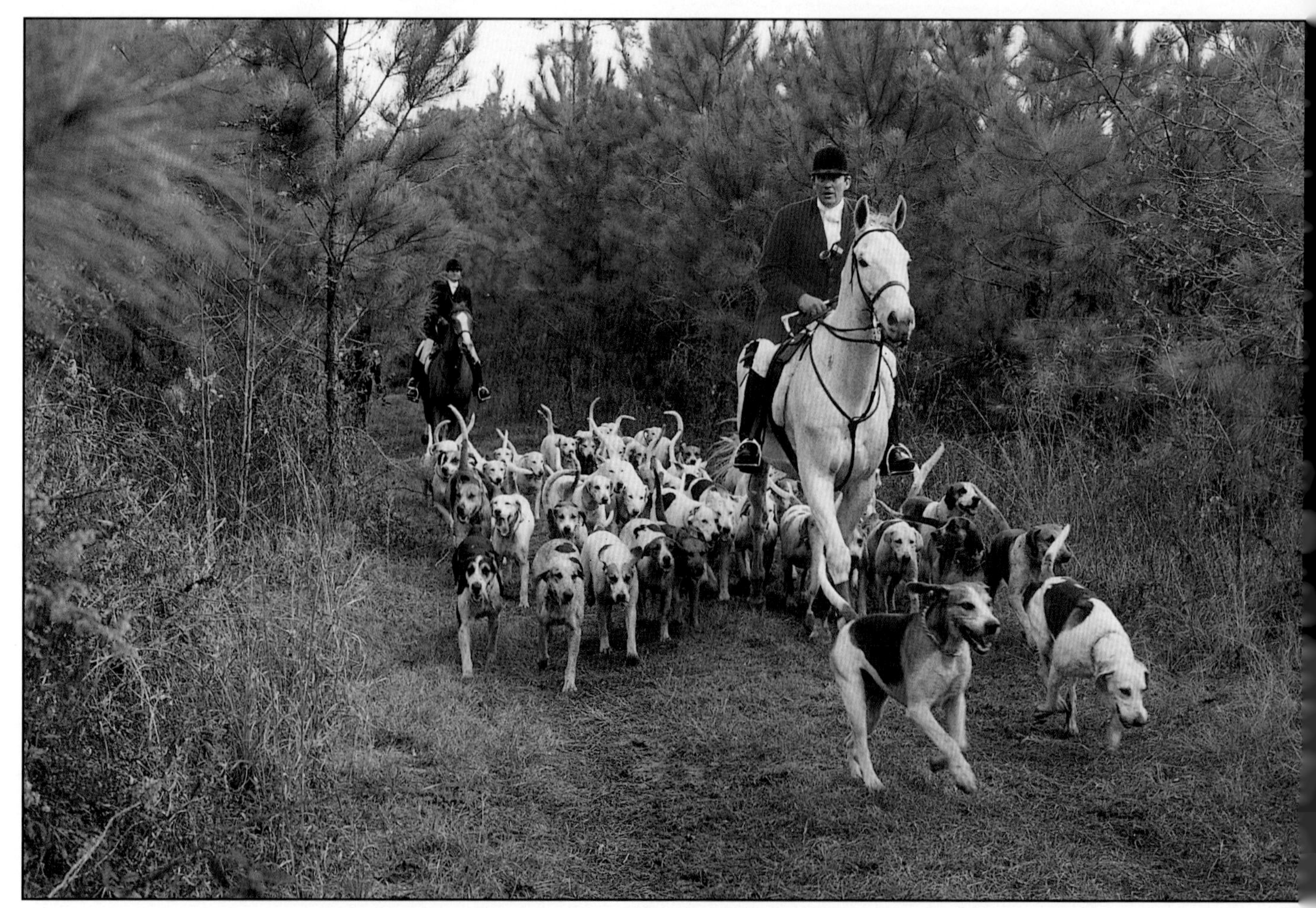

Founder joint master and huntsman to the Live Oak Hunt, Marty Wood, leading hounds out of 80 acre covert, after marking a big bob cat to ground.

L

The LIVE OAK *Hunt* (UNITED STATES OF AMERICA)

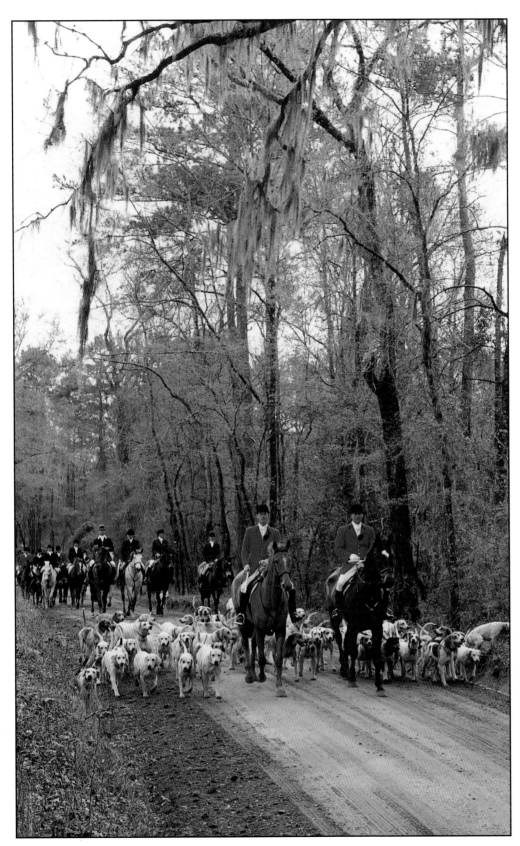

With the trees in Florida festooned with Spanish moss, the Live Oak hounds hack home at the end of a day's hunting. At the front are kennel huntsman Charles Montgomery and (left) whipper-in Dale Barnett. Heading the mounted field on the grey is joint master since 1976, Daphne Wood.

L

The
LLANARMON
Hunt
(MID WALES)

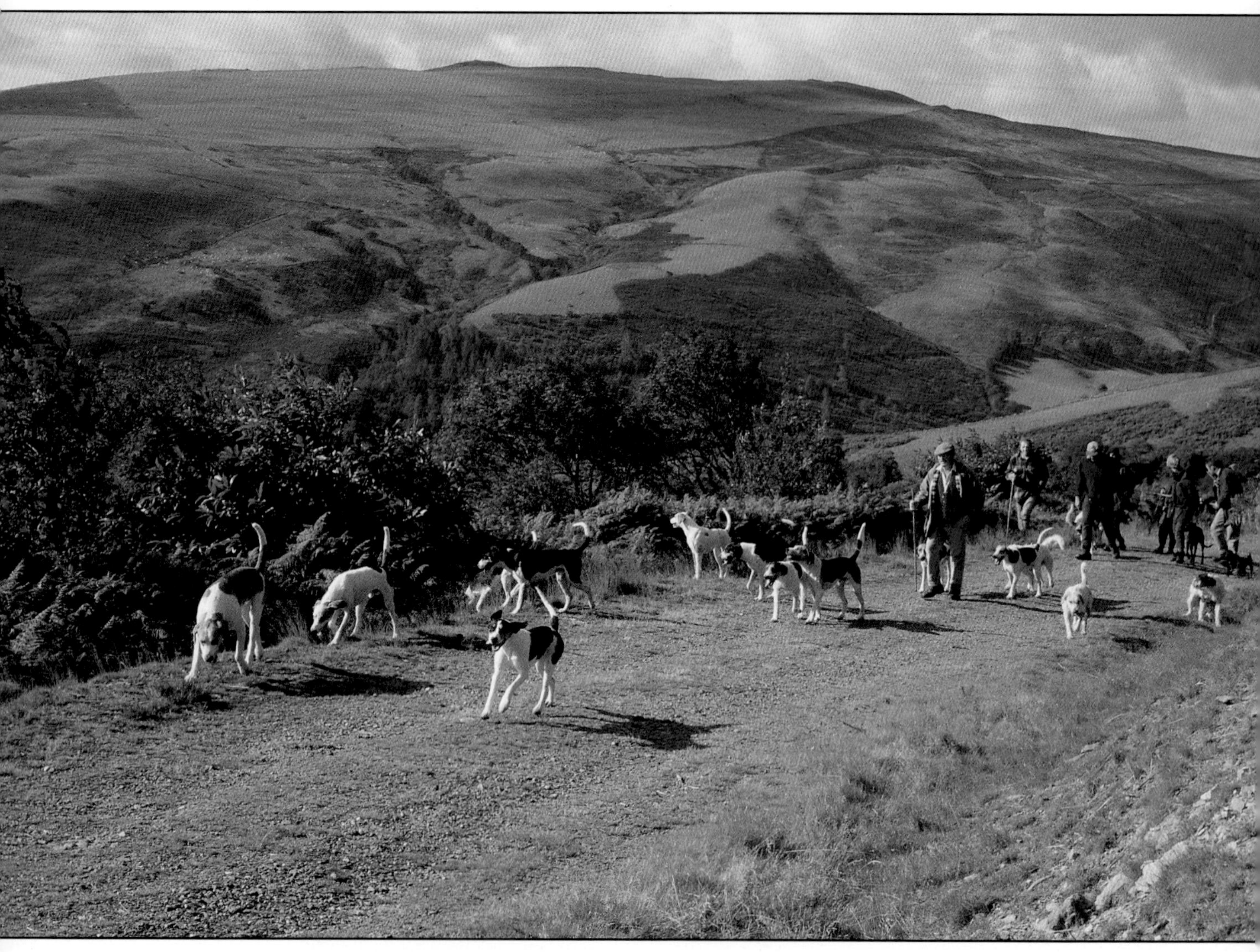

Huntsman Vic Matthews, who is also a gamekeeper, with the Llanarmon foxhounds, one of numerous small foot packs in Wales where the terrain is unsuitable for horses and where fox numbers have to be controlled.

The LONDON *Hunt* (CANADA)

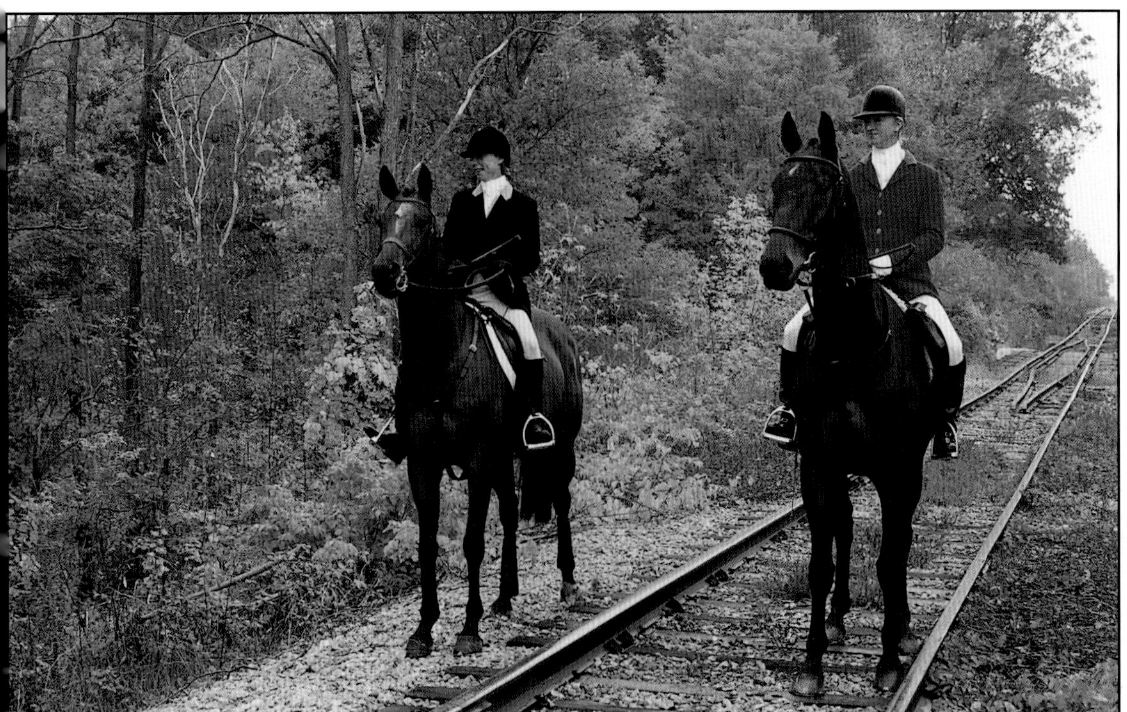

Sharon Holmes, whipper-in to the London Hunt, and Tina Luckhurst, whipper-in to the Hamilton Hunt, on point duty on a railway track in Canada.

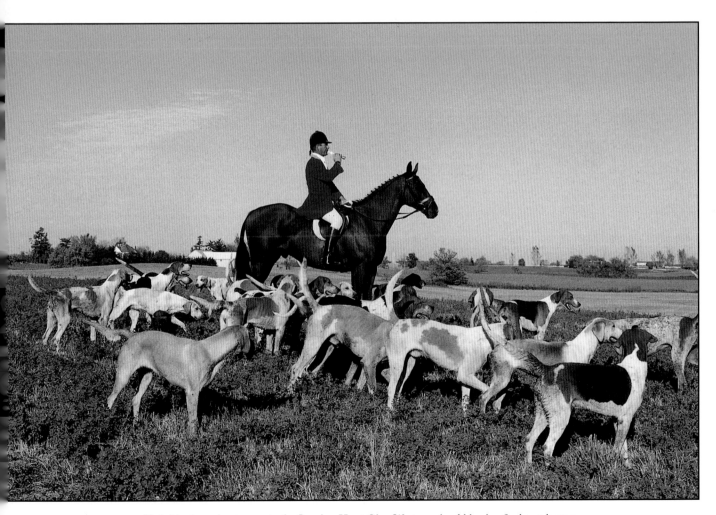

Yorkshire-born huntsman to the London Hunt Glen Westmoreland blowing for hounds on a sunny afternoon in late autumn.

L

LOWTHER HOUND SHOW PARADE

Lowther show's main ring filled with different types of foxhounds, during the spectacular grand finale and gallop at this popular north country show.

The LUDLOW *Hunt* (Shropshire, Herefordshire and Worcestershire)

With hounds as they hack to a meet at Downton Hall for an end of season occasion are L to R: Bill Andrewes - retiring MFH; Frances Meier - retiring MFH; David Palmer - retiring MFH and huntsman and Godfrey Berry - retiring kennel huntsman.

Joint master and huntsman to the Ludlow Hunt, Capt Rupert Inglesant, blowing for hounds after a good run from Downton Hall.

M

The
MIDDLETON HUNT CLUB
(UNITED STATES OF AMERICA)

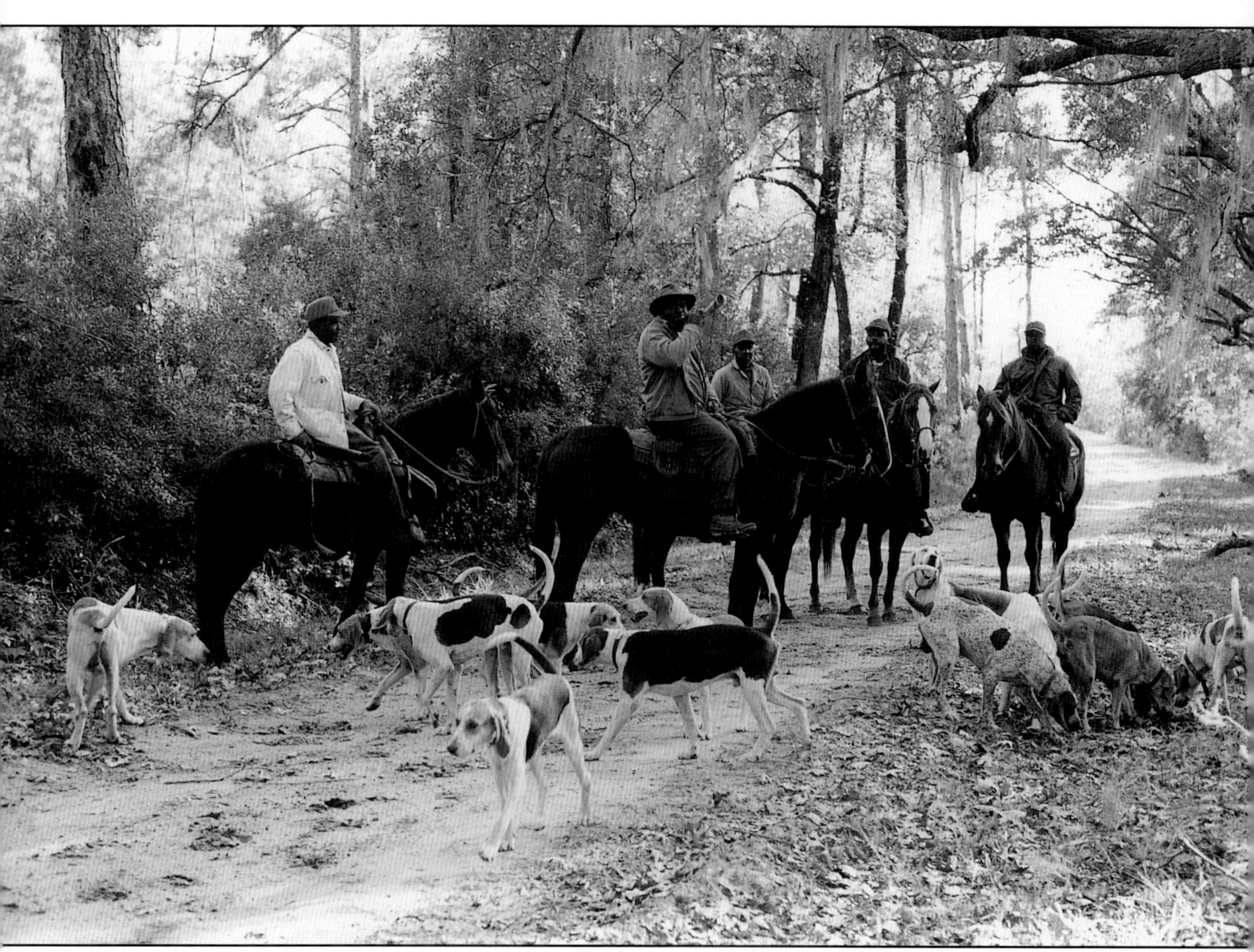

Staff of the Middleton Hunt Club, riding 'Marsh Tacky' ponies, collecting their American hounds after a hunt near Charleston, South Carolina, USA.

The MIDDLETON PLACE *Hunt*

(UNITED STATES OF AMERICA)

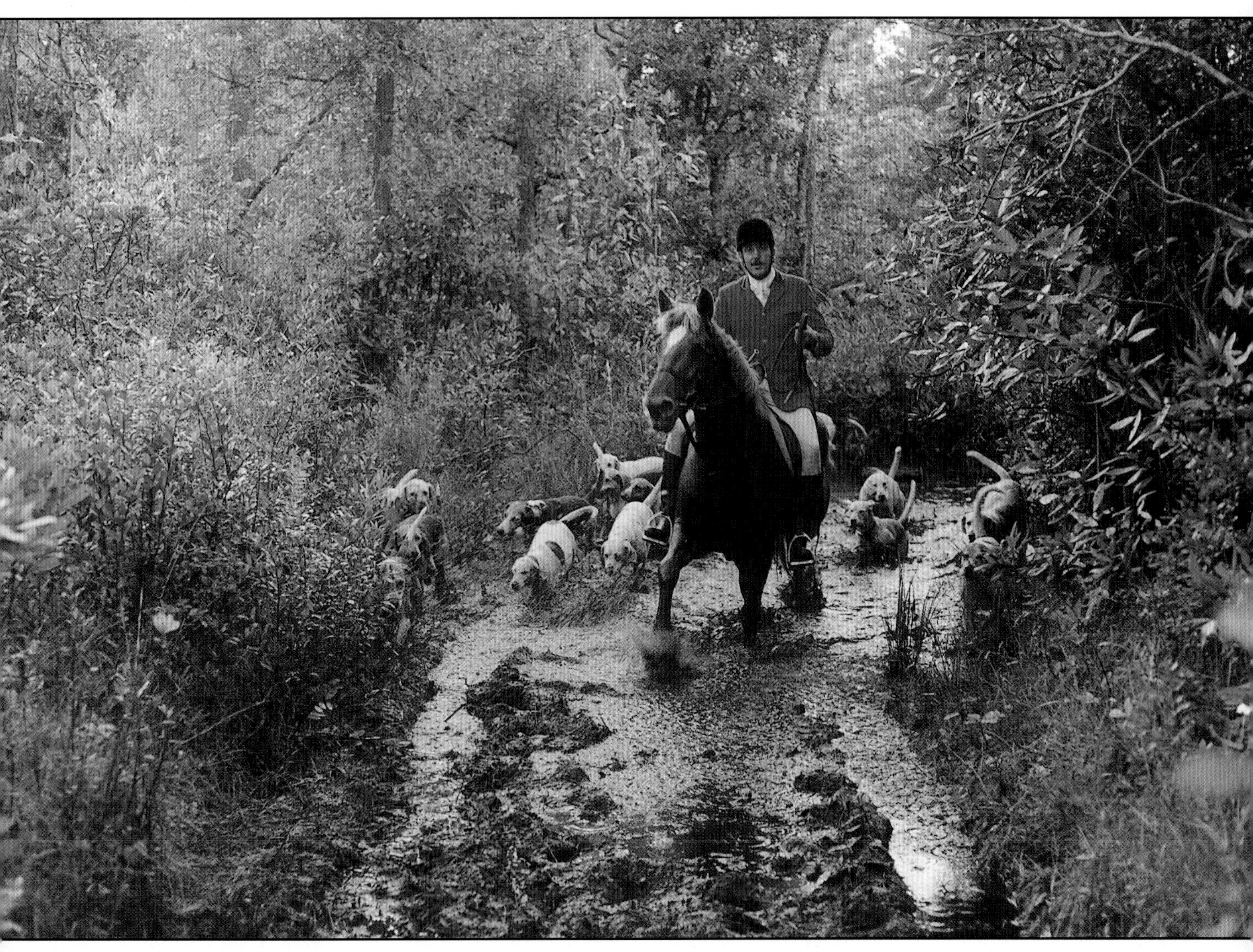

Kurt Krucke, huntsman to the Middleton Place hounds in South Carolina, leading his pack along a muddy track in a heavily wooded area.

The MIDLAND *Hunt* (UNITED STATES OF AMERICA)

The Midland hounds, with their founder joint master and huntsman Ben Hardaway III, waiting to move off from their meet at Hardaway Hall, only a short distance from the kennels at Midland, Georgia.

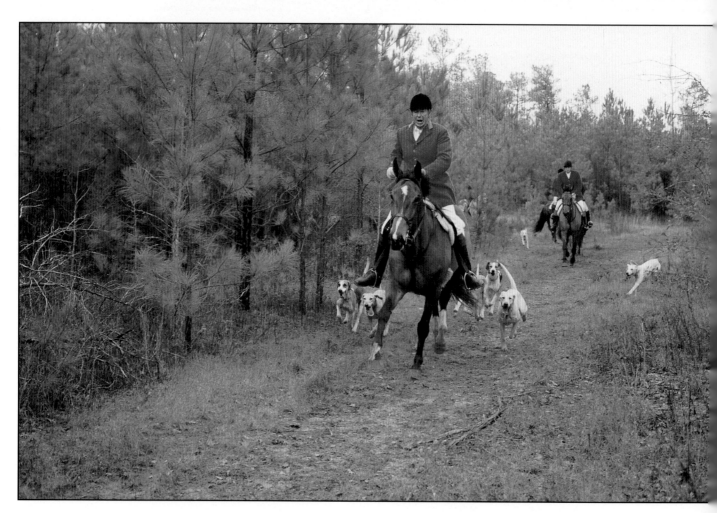

Ben Hardaway III, joint master and huntsman to the Midland Hunt since 1950, showing much enthusiasm as he encourages his hounds during a woodland hunt on a red fox.

The MIDLAND *Hunt* (UNITED STATES OF AMERICA)

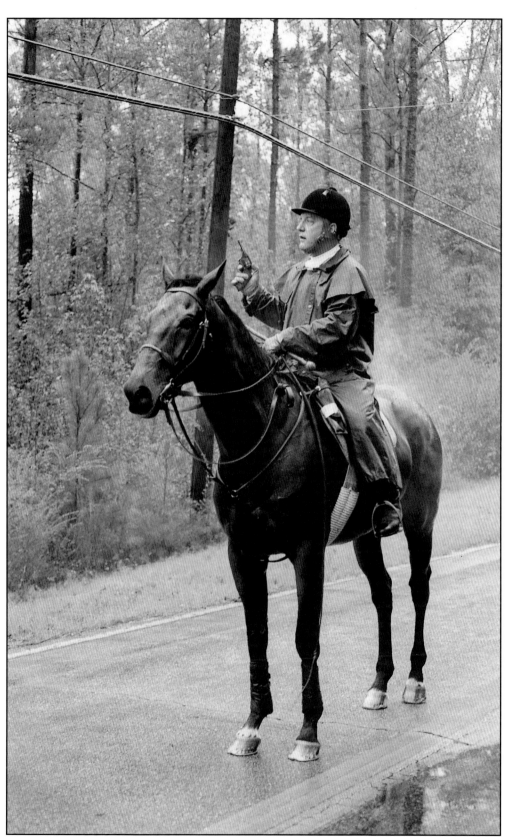

A very wet day at the Midland Hunt in Georgia, with a well wrapped up joint master Mason Lampton about to stop hounds from crossing a road, with a pistol – a normal happening with many American packs, especially when a coyote is being hunted.

M

MOTORISED QUAD-BIKES

Motorised quad bikes are the 'in thing' for modern day terrier men, as they can go almost anywhere without damaging even the softest and wettest grassland. Here after a joint meet are Terry Petrie from the Ludlow and Richard Jones, Warwickshire.

MOTORCYCLE FOLLOWERS

A group of motor cycle followers, at the end of a day with Sir Watkin Williams-Wynn's hounds. These are regular, knowledgeable and helpful hunt supporters, who are an asset to the hunt. Also in the group are terrier man Paul Connolly, kennel-huntsman Bert Loud and joint master Barrie Woolham.

M

The MYOPIA *Hunt* (UNITED STATES OF AMERICA)

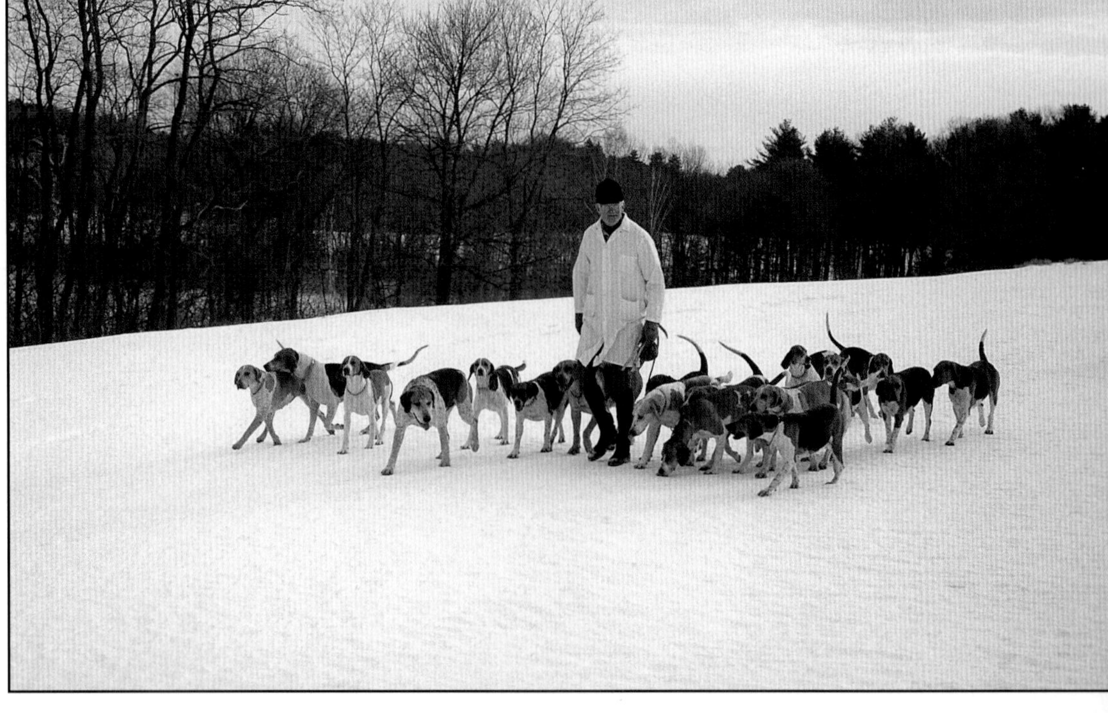

Russell Clark MFH, walking the Myopia hounds in the snow, close to the kennels at Hamilton, Massachusetts, during one of their severe winters.

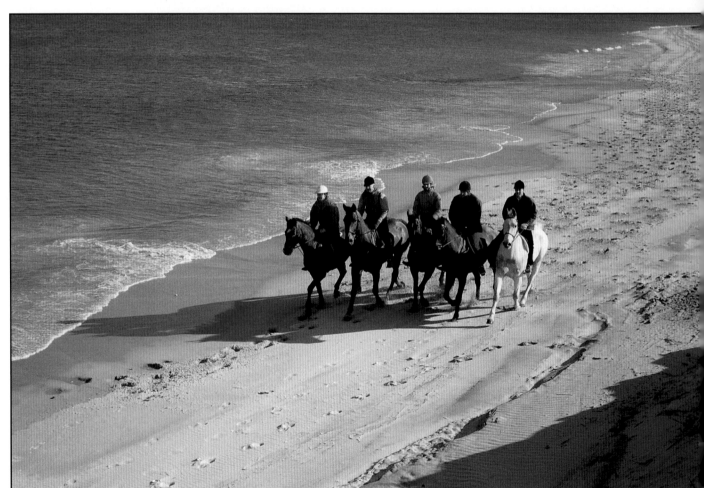

Myopia Hunt horses being exercised on Crane Beach, near Hamilton, Massachusetts, when the cold was so intense that salt spray from the sea was freezing on the sand.

The Burghley foxhounds, with their master and huntsman the Marquess of Exeter, were disbanded many years ago after a very short life.

Mrs Betty Gingell was master and huntsman to the Cambridgeshire Harriers from 1942-95, riding show hunters and giving great sport with her exceptional looking pack, which won innumerable championships at Peterborough.

Taking the Cheshire Forest hounds along a muddy lane at the start of the day are Philip Hunter, MFH and huntsman from 1947-76, and Sir Andrew Horsbrugh-Porter, the noted hunting correspondent for *The Field.*

The Cotley Harriers are owned by the Eames family and here Lt Col Dick Eames, master from 1939-87, takes his pack of white, west country harriers to draw from an opening meet at the family home at Cotley.

George Baskerville, who hunted the Modbury Harriers for so many years, pictured with his white west country hounds, above Modbury Village on the edge of Dartmoor.

Lord (Toby) Daresbury, here walking out the Old English Limerick hounds, was a master of the Belvoir from 1934-47 and of the Limerick from 1947-77. He also hunted these hounds from 1947-71. Following the pack are *Horse and Hound* editor Michael Clayton and Meriel Atkinson, who whipped-in to Lord Daresbury for many years.

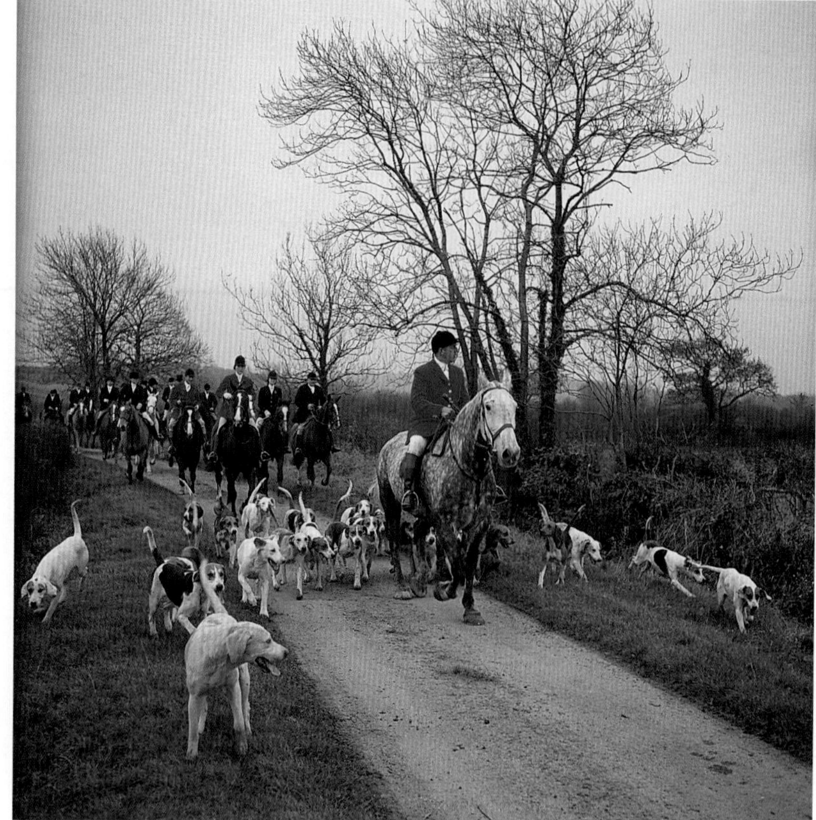

Derwent kennel-huntsman Claude Burton with hounds, followed by master and huntsman from 1946-74, Charles Chafer. With him are his daughters Pammy-Jane (now Mrs Ian Farquhar) in the red coat and Sally-Anne (now Mrs Neil Ewart).

The Galway Blazers hounds on the shore of Galway Bay, with master and huntsman from 1969-72, Capt Brian Fanshawe, followed by his whipper-in Henry Gordon. Hounds had been hunting on Tawin Island, where they accounted for a fox.

Lt Col Frank Mitchell and his wife Vecta were joint masters of the Hambledon Hunt before the amalgamation with the Hursley, with both hunting hounds.

The Linlithgow and Stirling Hunt, whose country was close to Edinburgh, seen here with huntsman Tom Potts just before they were disbanded due to urbanisation.

Sir Newton Rycroft, who was master of the New Forest Hunt from 1962-84, was a great hound breeder whose most famous hound was probably 'Medyg 69', by Plas Machynlleth 'Miller 63'. Sir Newton is pictured here with his pack on an open part of the forest, just prior to moving off.

The Scarteen (Black and Tans) are a unique pack of Kerry beagles, which have been hunted by the Ryan family for more than 300 years. Here Tommy O'Dwyer, kennel-huntsman since 1952, leads hounds from a meet at Elton with Thady Ryan, a master since 1946, following.

Mrs Elsie Morgan, who was joint master and huntsman to the West Waterford Hunt with her husband Tom from 1953-84, seen here with her pack of white hounds on the move across glorious Irish countryside.

Not only was Dorian Williams a master and top class field master to the Whaddon Chase Hunt from 1954-80, but he was also an internationally acclaimed radio and television commentator who specialised in show jumping.

The OAKLEY FOOT BEAGLES (LEICESTERSHIRE)

The Oakley Foot beagles, in spectacularly beautiful country in mid-Wales, being taken to draw by the joint masters David and Sarah Manning.

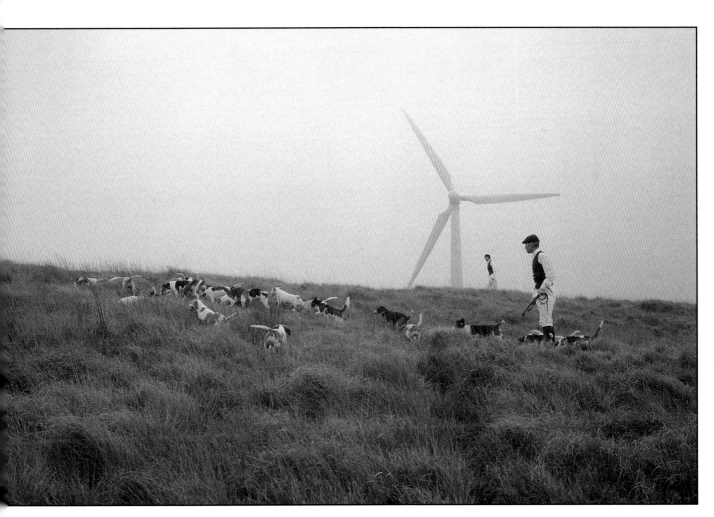

A huge and ghostly wind turbine looms out of the mist, as the Oakley Foot beagles and huntsman David Manning MH puzzle out the line during an early season hunt in mid-Wales. This is very different country to that which they normally hunt from their kennels in Leicestershire.

O

Mrs Jacqueline Kennedy ONASSIS

Mrs Jacqueline Kennedy Onassis with Ben Hardaway III MFH at a meet of the Midland hounds in Virginia during the match with the Piedmont Hunt. Mrs Onassis hunted on six out of the seven days of this most exciting competition.

America's former First Lady jumping a stone wall at the front of the mounted field during a hunt in the Piedmont country, Virginia, USA.

The ORANGE COUNTY *Hunt* (UNITED STATES OF AMERICA)

Senior master to the Orange County Hunt since 1982, Jimmy Young, who is also field master, leads the way over a coop. He was president of the American MFHA from 1993-96.

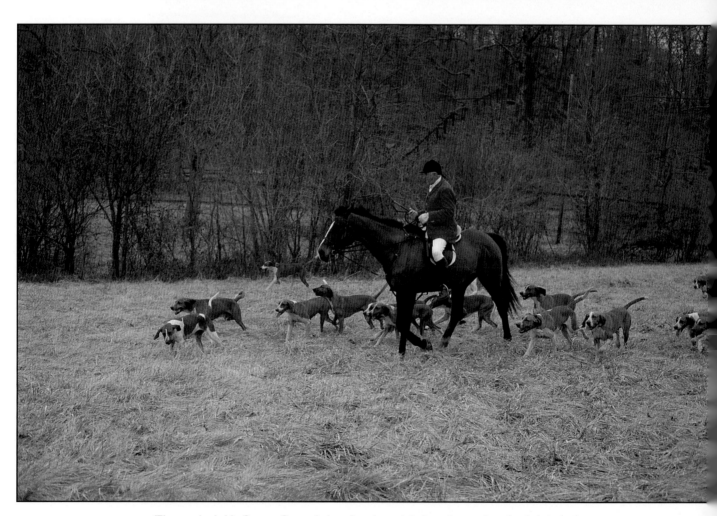

The unmistakable Orange County's American hounds being taken to draw by their long time huntsman Melvin Poe, in Virginia, USA.

The Dumfriesshire Otterhounds, with huntsman Will Scott, working a big Scottish river.

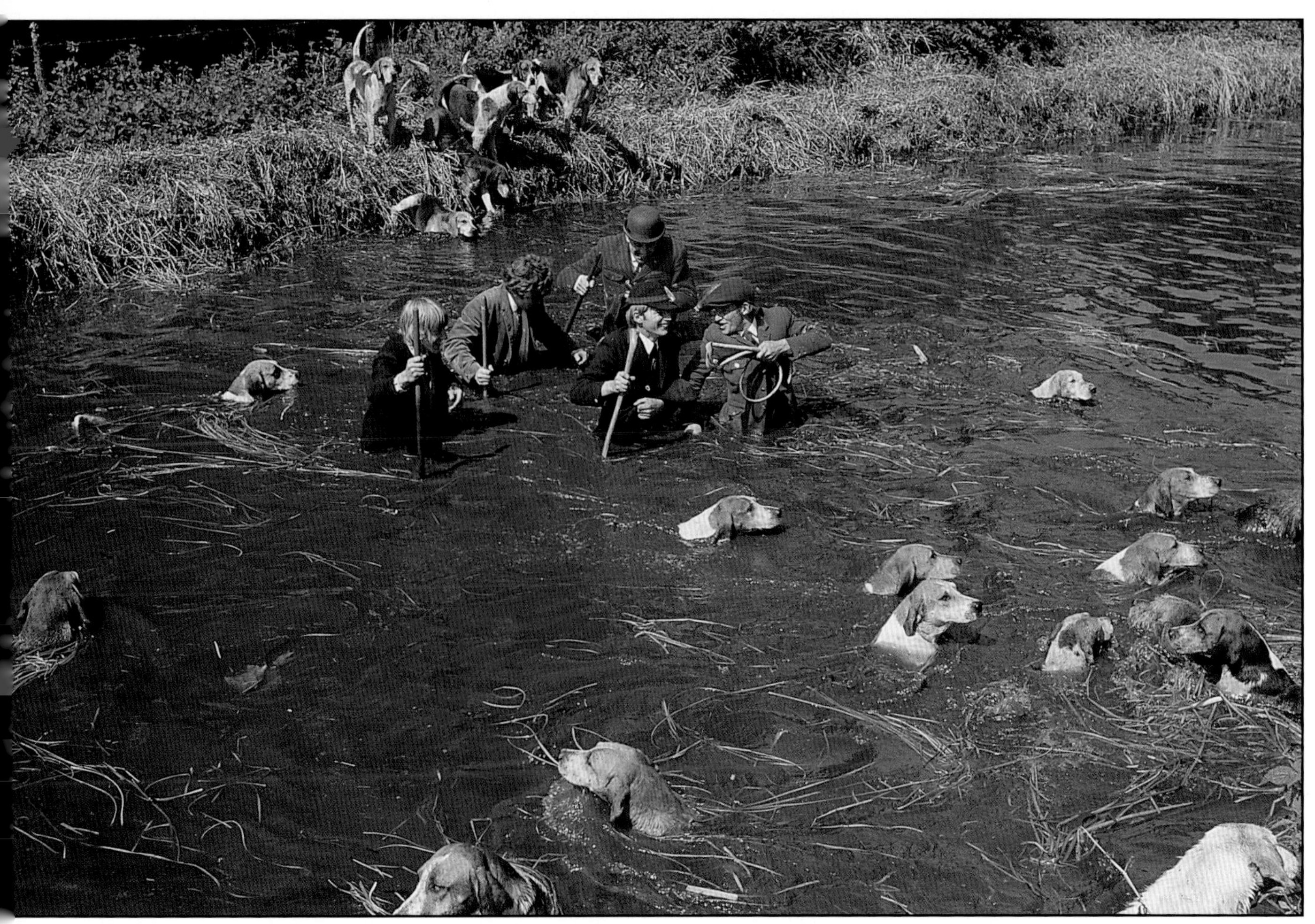

In uniform, as the Eastern Counties Otterhounds cross a weed-strewn river, are Michael Farrow, Michael Sagar and Derek Gardiner. From the smiles, they all appear to be enjoying themselves immensely!

OTTERHOUNDS

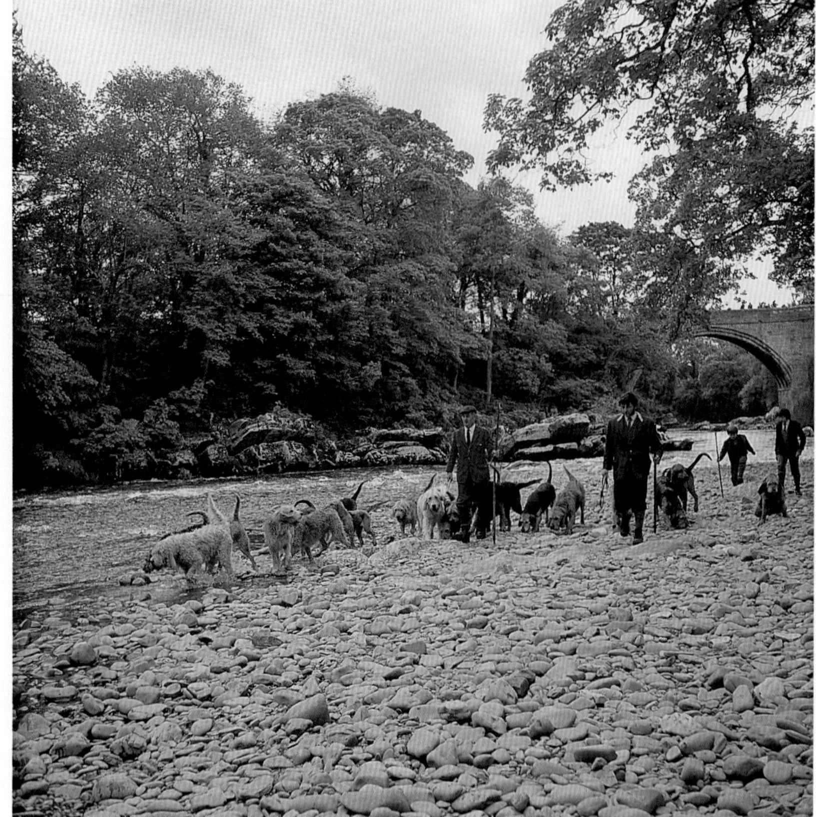

Well known huntsman Tommy Harrison leading his pack of pure bred Kendal and District otterhounds over a rocky area on the River Lune.

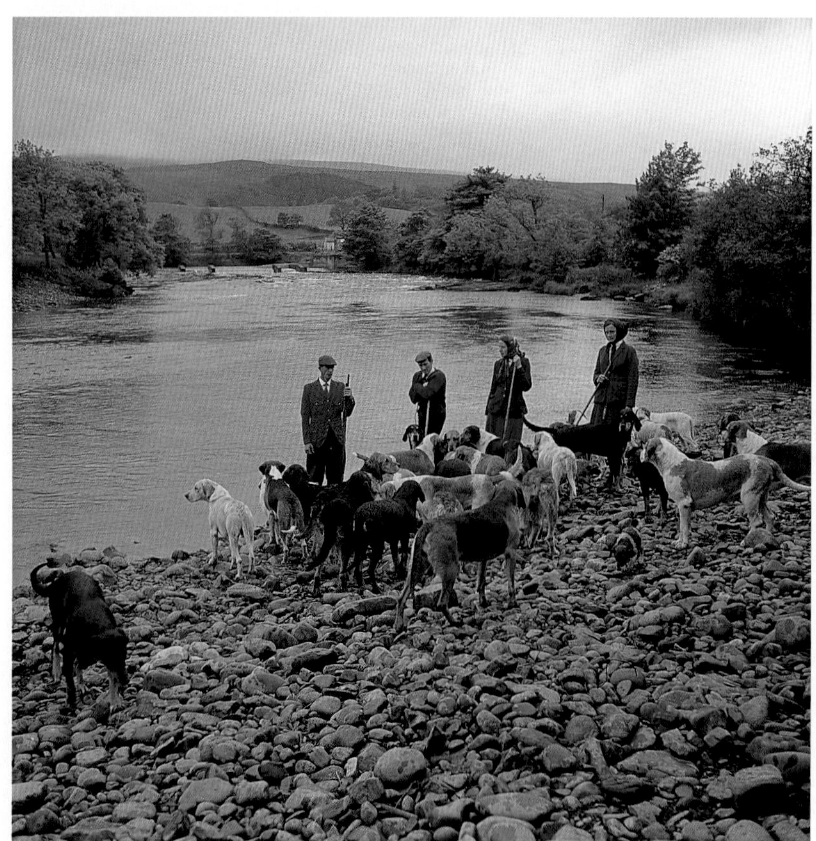

With the Northern Counties Otterhounds, as they wait to begin drawing, are (in uniform) huntsman Lionel Douse, whipper-in Sarah Dove and the master June Paisley.

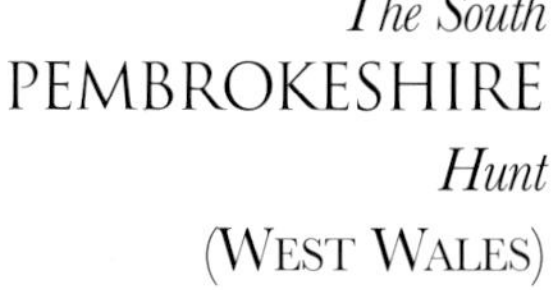

The South PEMBROKESHIRE *Hunt* (WEST WALES)

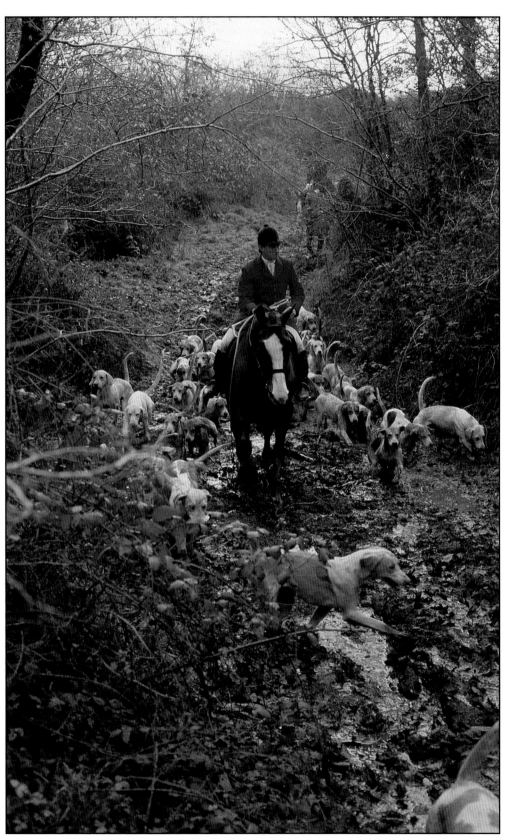

The South Pembrokeshire hounds with Simon Hart, who was joint master and huntsman from 1988-98, making their way along a wet and muddy lane in West Wales. Despite being a Welsh pack, their hounds are very much 'modern' English.

The PENDLE FOREST AND CRAVEN HARRIERS (LANCASHIRE AND YORKSHIRE)

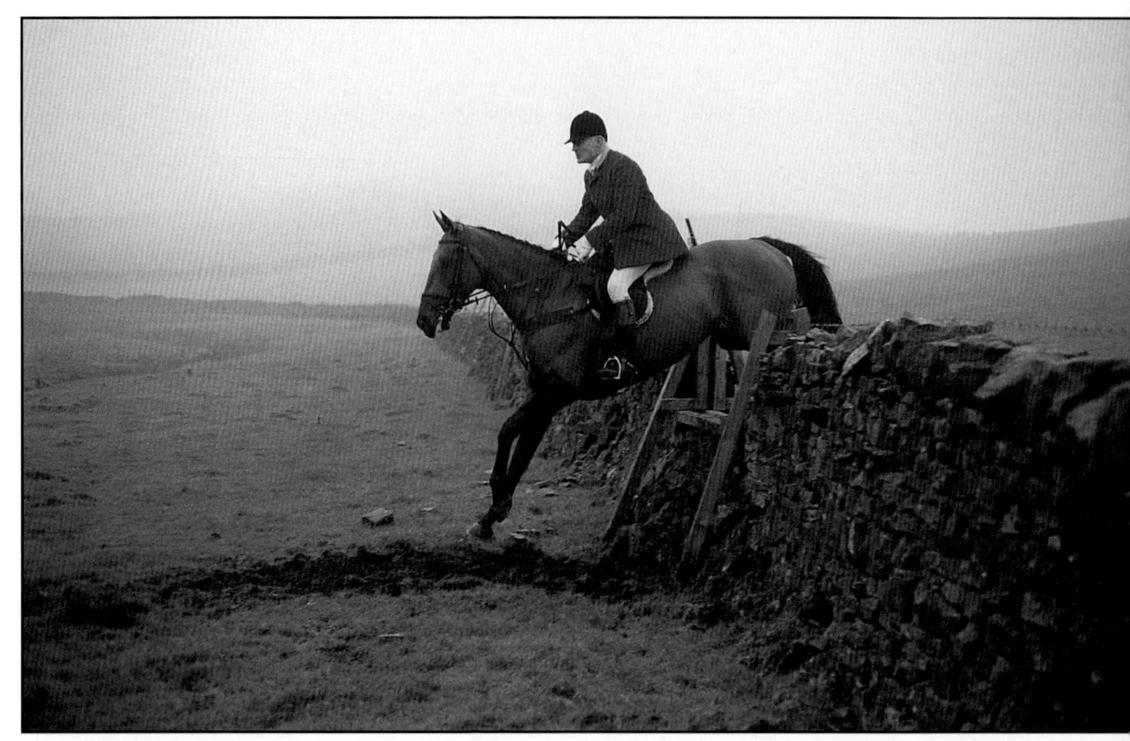

Michael Bannister, a joint master of the Pendle Forest and Craven Harriers since 1977, clearing a jumping place in a typical tall stone wall.

A misty morning in the hills as Richard Lloyd, huntsman to the Pendle Forest and Craven Harriers, takes hounds to draw in this all grass country on the borders of Lancashire and North Yorkshire.

The PERCY *Hunt* (NORTHUMBERLAND)

Huntsman Don Claxton leading the Percy hounds along the River Aln with Alnwick Castle, ancestral home of the masters, the Dukes of Northumberland, towering high above. The present masters are the 12th Duke and his sister, Lady Victoria Cuthbert, with hounds being hunted by Don Claxton's son Martin.

PETERBOROUGH ROYAL FOXHOUND SHOW

The Prince of Wales arriving at the show, accompanied by the Earl and Countess Fitzwilliam MFH, in 1978 when he was show president.

Queen Elizabeth, the Queen Mother, with Lt Col Tony Murray-Smith MFH and Ken Goschen MFH, admiring the Vale of Aylesbury hounds with their long serving huntsman Jim Bennett.

PETERBOROUGH ROYAL FOXHOUND SHOW

Princess Anne talking in the ring with the Duke of Beaufort MFH and Sir Philip Naylor-Leyland MFH (left) who is the show chairman.

The Duchess of Gloucester leaving the show with Sir Stephen Hastings MFH, passing hounds preparing to enter the collecting ring.

P

The

PIC'ARDIE VALOIS BUCKHOUNDS

(FRANCE)

A bitterly cold day, in France's forest of Compiègne, as the équipage Pic'Ardie Valois black and white hounds are brought home at the end of the day, to the accompaniment of much horn blowing.

The PIEDMONT *Hunt* (UNITED STATES OF AMERICA)

Piedmont hounds at summer exercise from their kennels near Upperville, with joint master and huntsman Randy Waterman, a former top point to point rider.

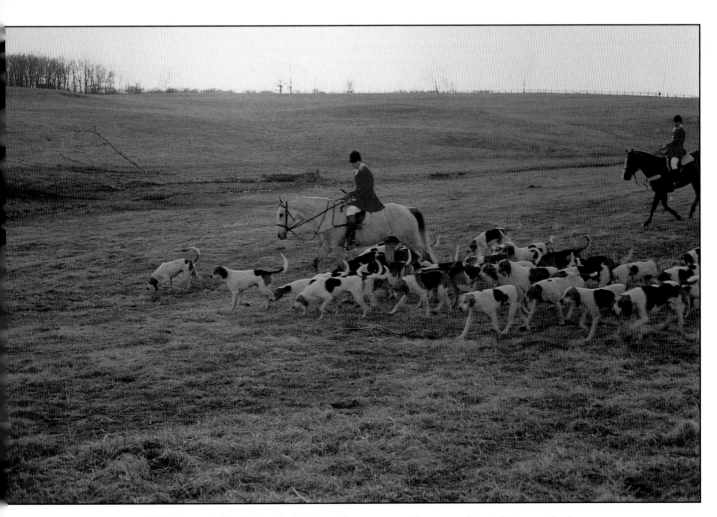

With the sun sinking below the horizon, joint master and huntsman Randy Waterman leads the Piedmont hounds back to the boxes, following a splendid day's hunting in this well organised grass country in Virginia, only 40 miles west of Washington D.C.

The
PLUM RUN
Hunt
(UNITED STATES OF AMERICA)

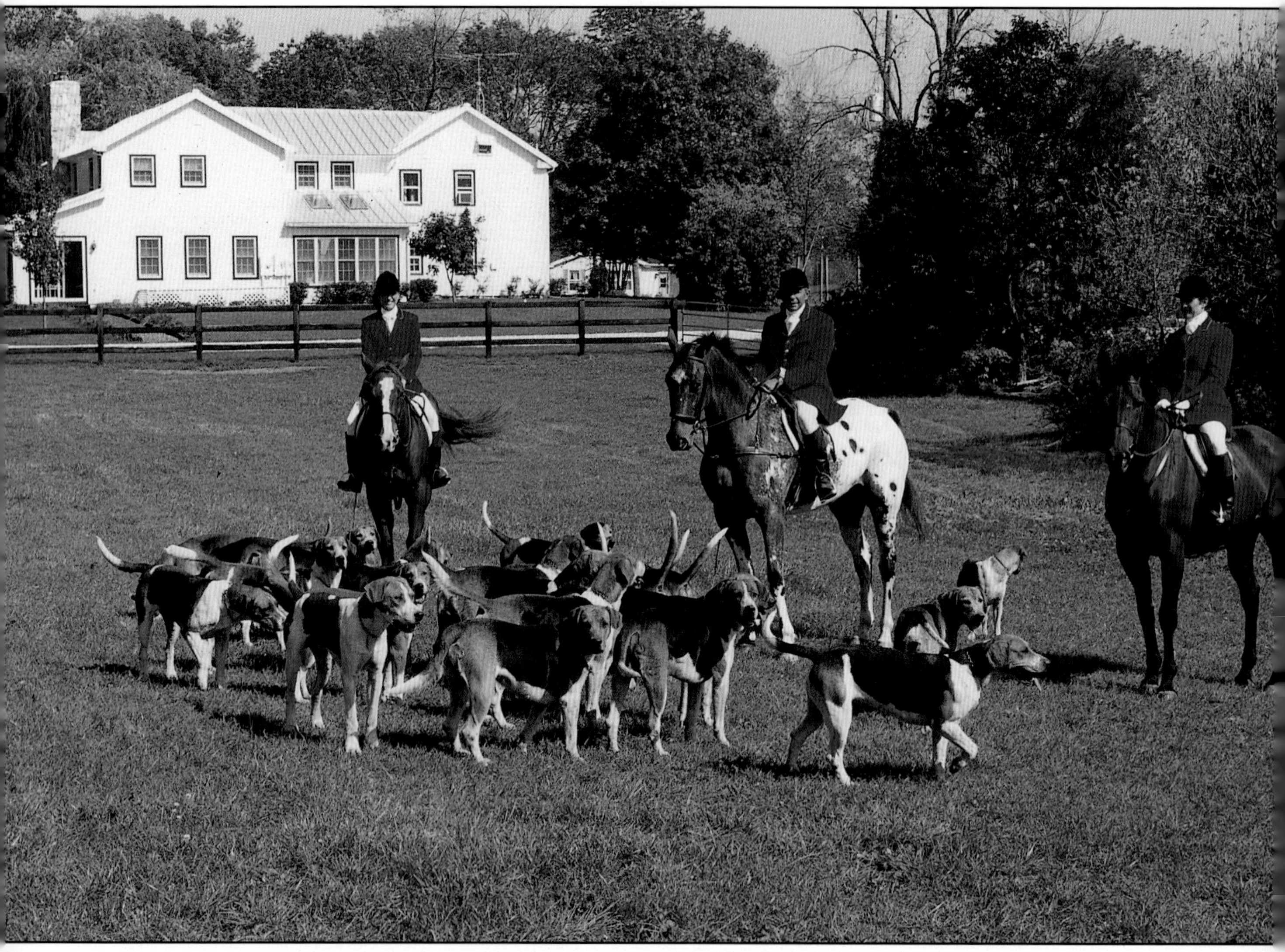

The only pack of Old English foxhounds in America, the Plum Run, seen here in front of their club house not far from Gettysburg, Pennsylvania. In uniform are (right to left) Miss Suzy Reingold, senior master; Robert Dougherty MFH and huntsman; and Diane Dougherty - hon sec.

The POTOMAC *Hunt* (UNITED STATES OF AMERICA)

With mist rising from a lake, the Potomac hounds, with huntsman Larry Pitts, awaiting the order to move off from an early morning meet at the kennels in Maryland.

HRH PRINCE CHARLES

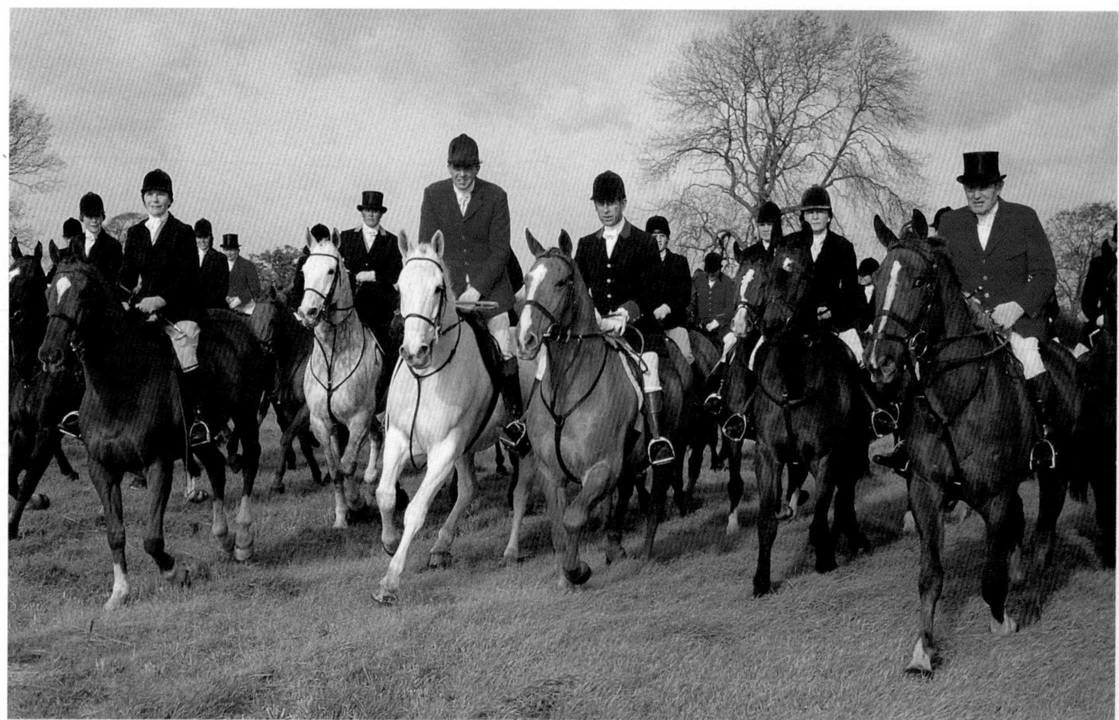

Heading the Quorn field, between Jim Bealby MFH and his wife Sue.

With huntsman Michael Farrin, taking the Quorn bitches to draw in the Monday country.

HRH PRINCE CHARLES

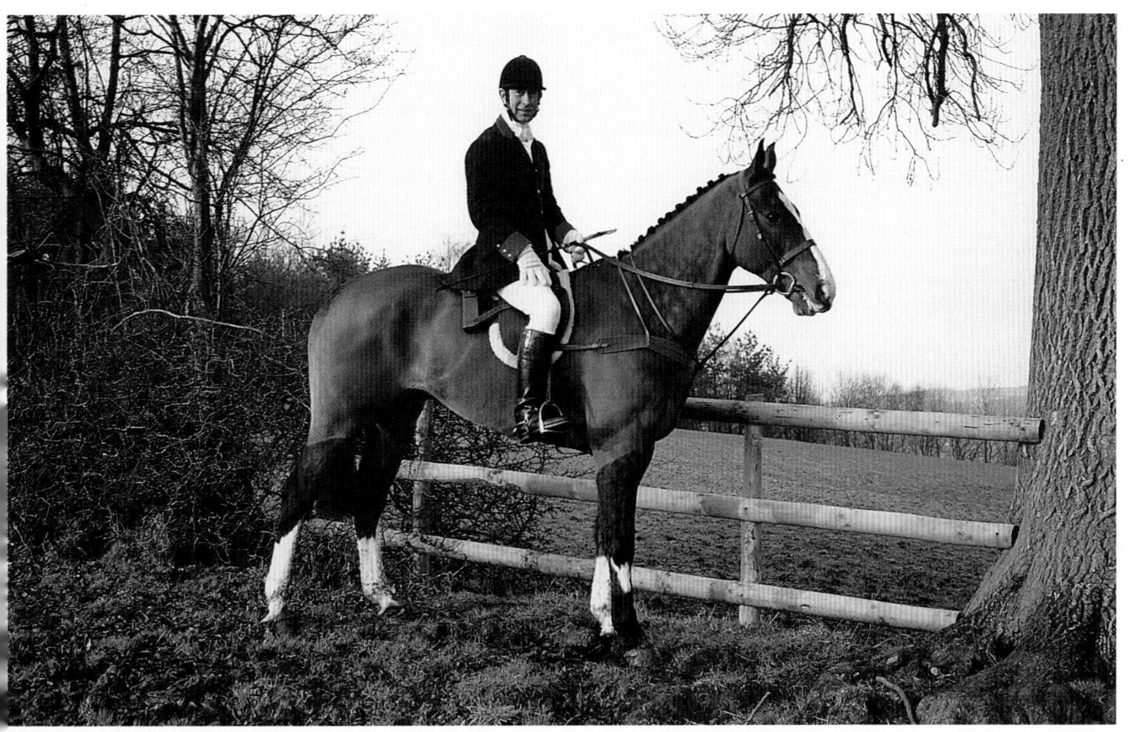

Immaculate in his Windsor livery, the Prince of Wales on point duty during an excellent day's hunting with the Meynell.

Clearing a big Meynell hedge, in an endeavour to keep huntsman David Barker in sight.

P

HRH

PRINCE CHARLES

Away from Muxlow Hill, in the Quorn country.

'The People's Prince' surrounded by knowledgeable foot followers, on point at Curates Covert from where many good hunts have begun.

Home! Hacking hounds home at the end of a splendid day with the Meynell, in company with huntsmen David Barker and Michael Farrin. Both of these top huntsmen have now retired; Michael Farrin in 1998 and David Barker in 1999.

P

PUPPY SHOWS

A perfect summer's day at Badminton, as Capt Brian Fanshawe and Martin Scott judge the Duke of Beaufort's young entry, shown by kennel-huntsman Charles Wheeler.

The Duke of Rutland's Belvoir kennels provide an unchanging background as Nicholas Soames MP and Brian Gupwell sort out the young bitches, produced by huntsman Martin Thornton.

PUPPY SHOWS

Meynell huntsman David Barker on the flags with his bitch entry, being judged by Lindsay Wallace and Tom Normington.

A very wet day at the Puckeridge kennels as kennel-huntsman Tim Edwards shows the young hounds to the judges, Major John Berkeley and Willie Poole.

The
PYTCHLEY
Hunt
(NORTHAMPTONSHIRE AND LEICESTERSHIRE)

Wearing the distinctive Padua red coat with white collar is Pytchley huntsman since 1971, Peter Jones. He and his whipper-in Richard Emmott, on the grey, are leading hounds across country after an early opening meet, with the country still very 'green'.

The PYTCHLEY *Hunt*
(NORTHAMPTONSHIRE AND LEICESTERSHIRE)

The Pytchley hounds hunting slowly away from De Traffords covert at dusk, just before 'Home' was blown as the light faded with only a dozen or so riders still out.

Q

The
QUORN
Hunt
(HIGH LEICESTERSHIRE)

After heavy overnight rain, the Quorn hounds found scenting conditions to their liking as they raced away down a hedgerow, with tremendous drive and cry, in hot pursuit of a fox only one minute in front.

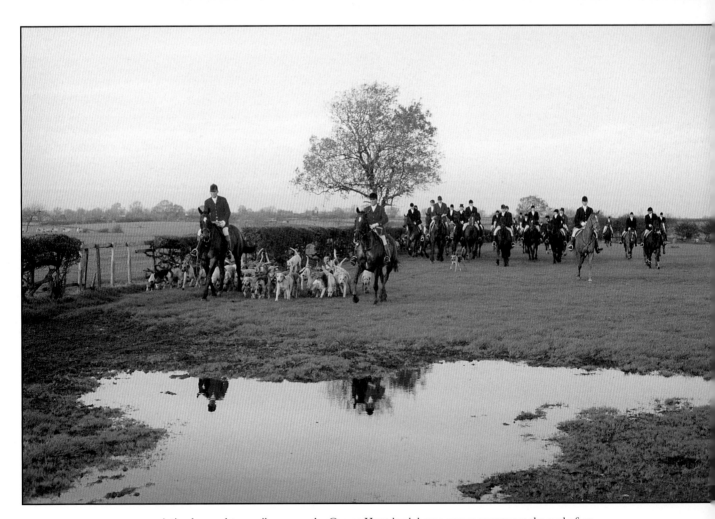

A timeless and tranquil scene as the Quorn Hunt hack home across country at the end of an outstanding day in the Monday country. With hounds is Michael Farrin, huntsman 1968-98, while on the chestnut is Prince Charles.

The RADNOR AND WEST HEREFORDSHIRE *Hunt*

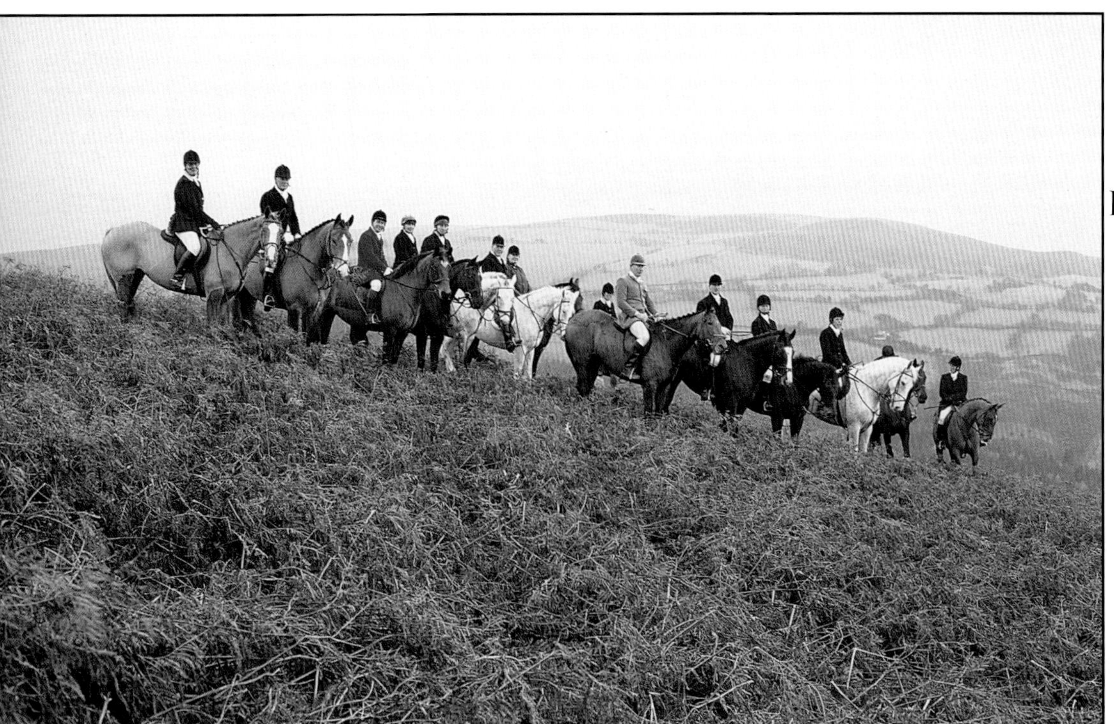

The field on a bracken covered hillside, watching as hounds draw below them.

Radnor and West Herefordshire huntsman David Morgan, with his hounds on Llanfaredd Hill, after meeting in Builth Wells during the Welsh Hunt week, when a different pack meets at the Barley Mow every day of the week.

R

RAINBOW

It is not often that the opportunity occurs to photograph a rainbow during a day's hunting. However, it did happen when I was out with the Brocklesby Hunt in Lincolnshire, as the field watched hounds draw.

The RAPPAHANNOCK *Hunt* (UNITED STATES OF AMERICA)

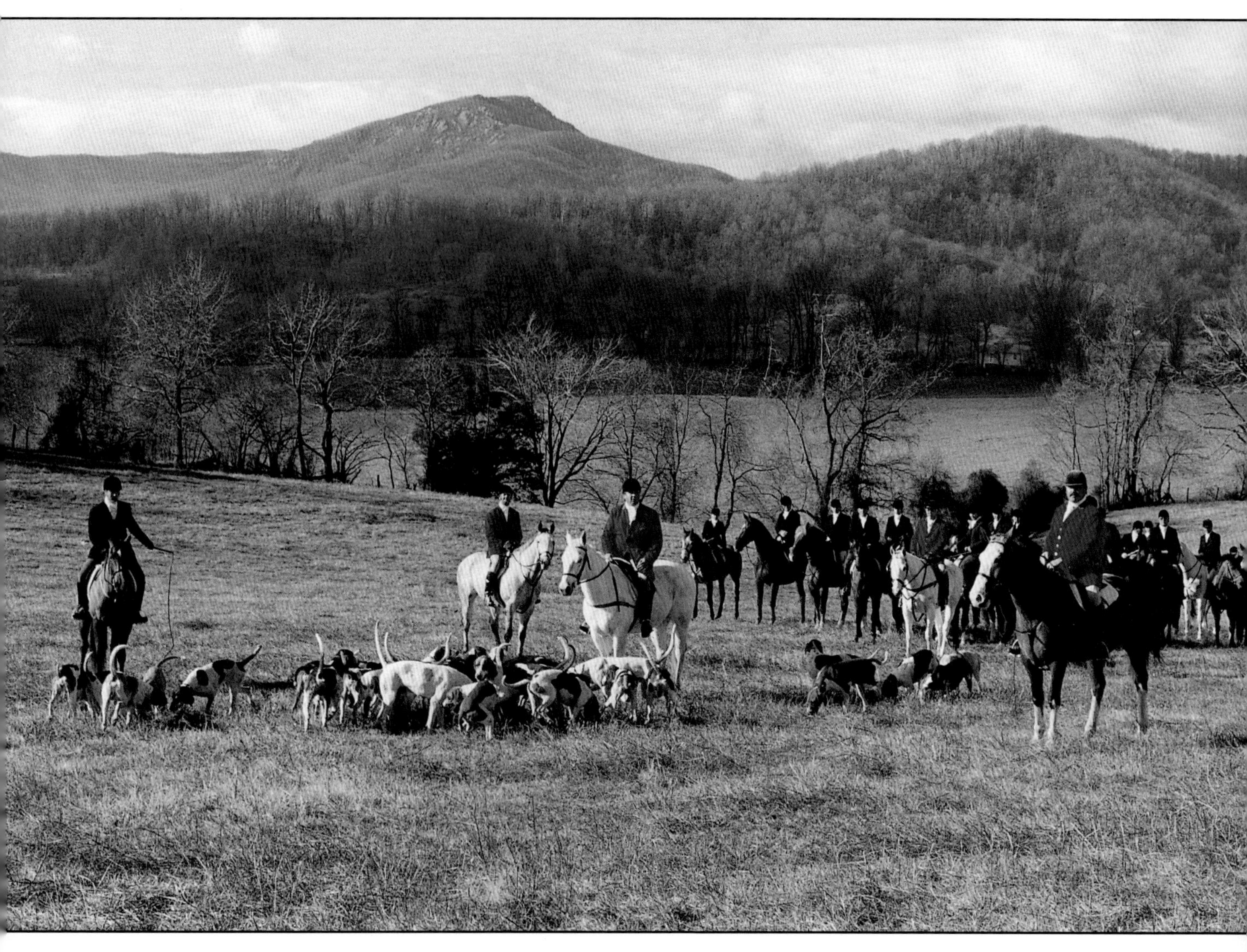

Amidst spectacular scenery, the Rappahannock hounds meet not far from their kennels at Sperryville, Virginia. Centre, with the pack, is huntsman Oliver Brown, about to give the order to move off.

RECORD

Betty McKeever, who was master of the Blean Beagles for a record 81 years, from 1909-90, pictured here with Capt. Ronnie Wallace MFH and huntsman Nick Valentine with hounds at her 70th opening meet.

R

REFLECTIONS

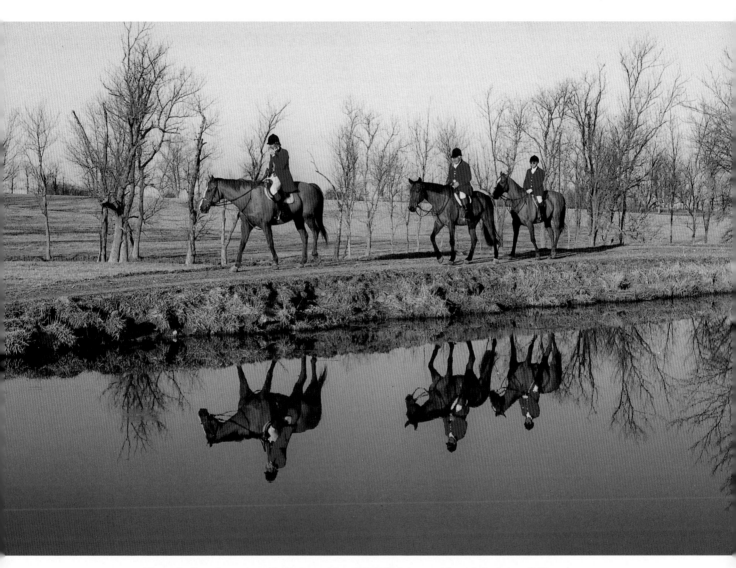

Not a ripple to be seen on Dr Jack van Nagell MFH's lake, as riders of the Iroquois Hunt in Kentucky hack home at the end of the day, following a lawn meet at Brookfield Farm.

REPAIRS

Dick Threadgold, the Pytchley Hunt's fencing man, repairing a fence which had been damaged during a hunt and was no longer stock proof. This is of major importance in maintaining good relations with farmers over whose land the mounted field ride.

Tim Fitton, enjoying a good hunt with the Pendle Forest and Craven Harriers, still found time to stop and rebuild a stone wall which had been knocked down by the field as they jumped it.

Michael Farrin leading the Quorn hounds home for the very last time, at the end of a brilliant 30 years career as huntsman to this top Leicestershire pack, on 18 March 1998.

R

ROCKY COUNTRY

Rocky outcrops litter the ground in a gorse covert, as followers of the Kilmoganny Hunt in County Kilkenny watch hounds at work.

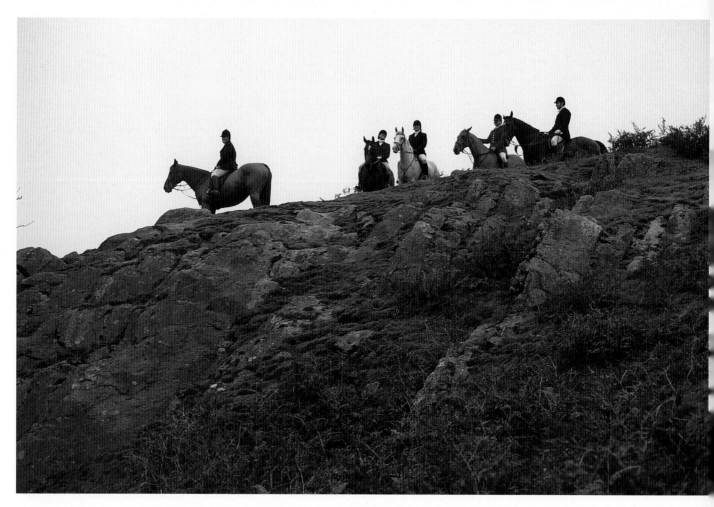

Rocky cliffs on a steep hillside near to the Welsh borders, as the field of the Tanatside Hunt avoid going too close to the edge, below which hounds were drawing.

The ROYAL AGRICULTURAL COLLEGE BEAGLES (GLOUCESTERSHIRE)

The Royal Agricultural College beagles moving off from a meet at the college, situated on the outskirts of Cirencester. Master and huntsman Charles Frampton is with hounds and he went on to be joint master and huntsman of the Bedale foxhounds, at the age of 21!

SNOW

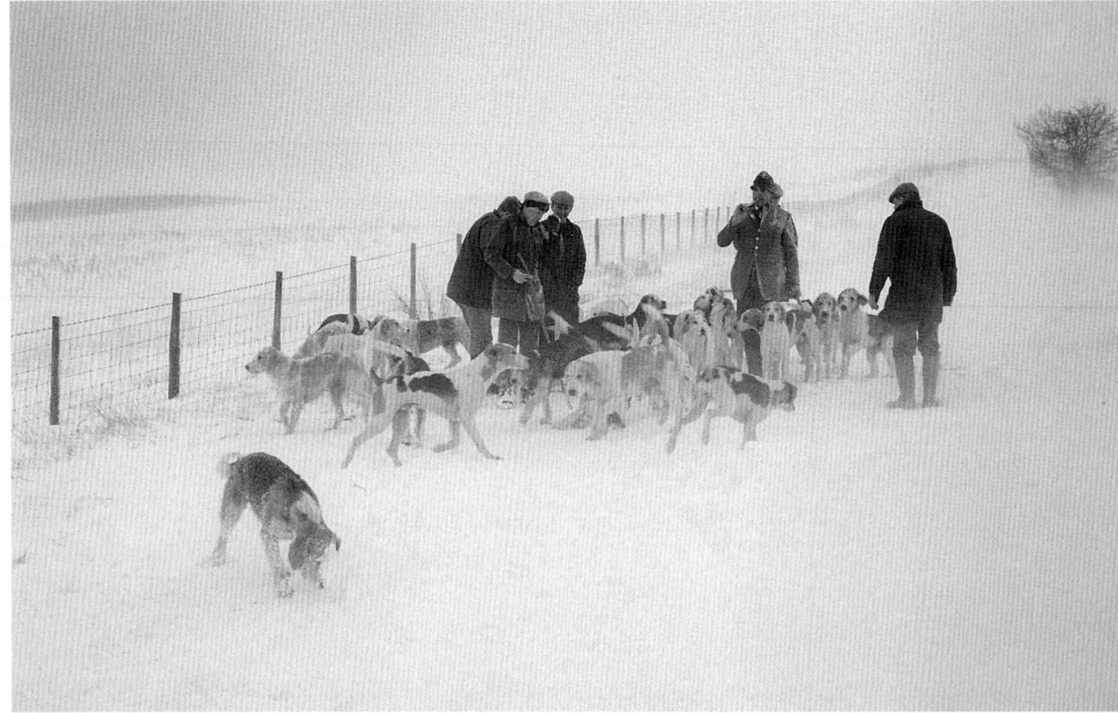

The David Davies hounds being collected in white out conditions, as a blizzard struck after a hunt to Blue Lynx.

The Lunesdale hounds over 2,000 feet up in the Lake District fells, with long time huntsman John Nicholson.

Huntsman Hugh Robards taking his old English Limerick foxhounds to draw, after an overnight fall of snow in Ireland.

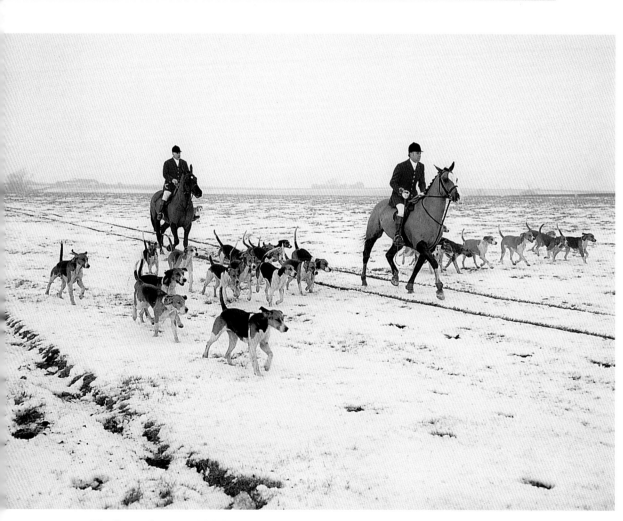

The Burton hounds, which hunt in Lincolnshire, on a snowy day, with huntsman since 1967 Jim Lang and Arthur Lockwood, master from 1959-99, who enjoyed a most successful partnership.

SNOW

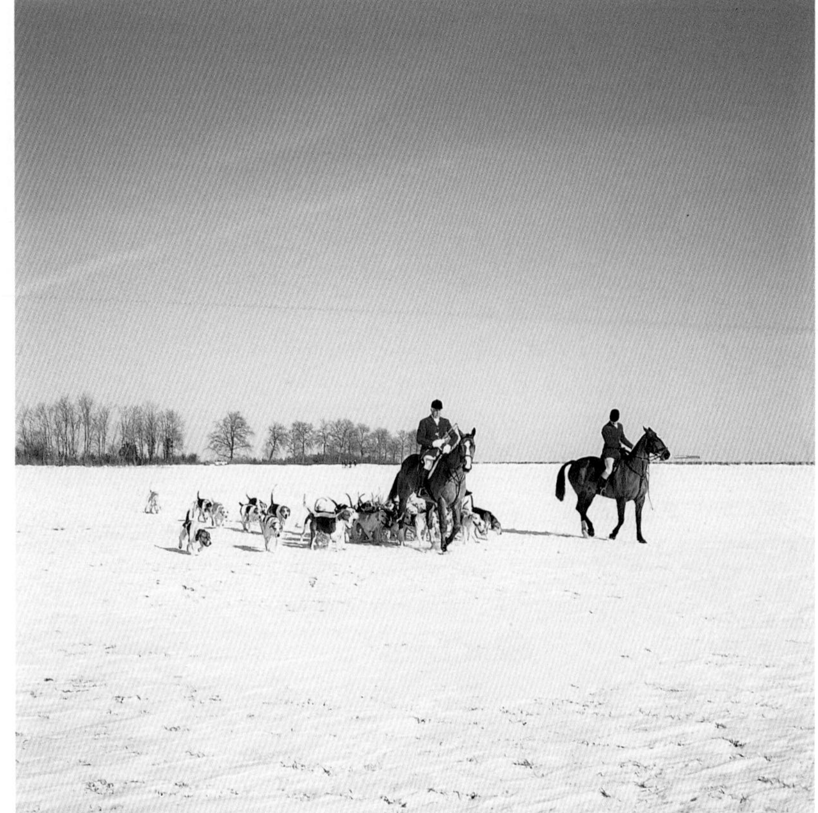

On a veritable prairie of snow, the Oakley hounds with Harold Bowley MFH and huntsman during an entertaining day's hunting in Bedfordshire.

Huntsman Tom Batterbee with his Suffolk hounds near Long Melford, on a day which was interrupted by a blizzard and brought to a premature end.

The SOUTH CREEK *Hunt* (UNITED STATES OF AMERICA)

The South Creek foxhounds, led by huntsman Robert Douglas, moving off from a misty meet near Tampa, Florida, USA.

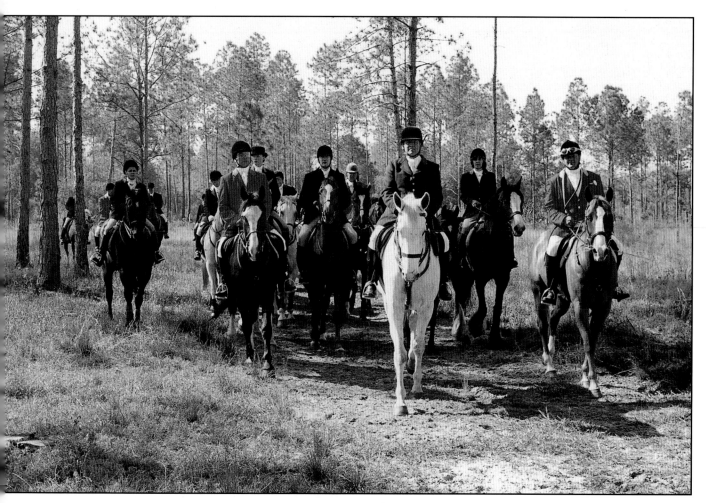

Rick Michaels, joint master of the South Creek foxhounds in Florida and the County Clare Hunt in Ireland, heading the field during a day's hunting near Tampa, Florida. He is wearing his County Clare livery, which features a green coat.

The SOUTH SHROPSHIRE *Hunt*

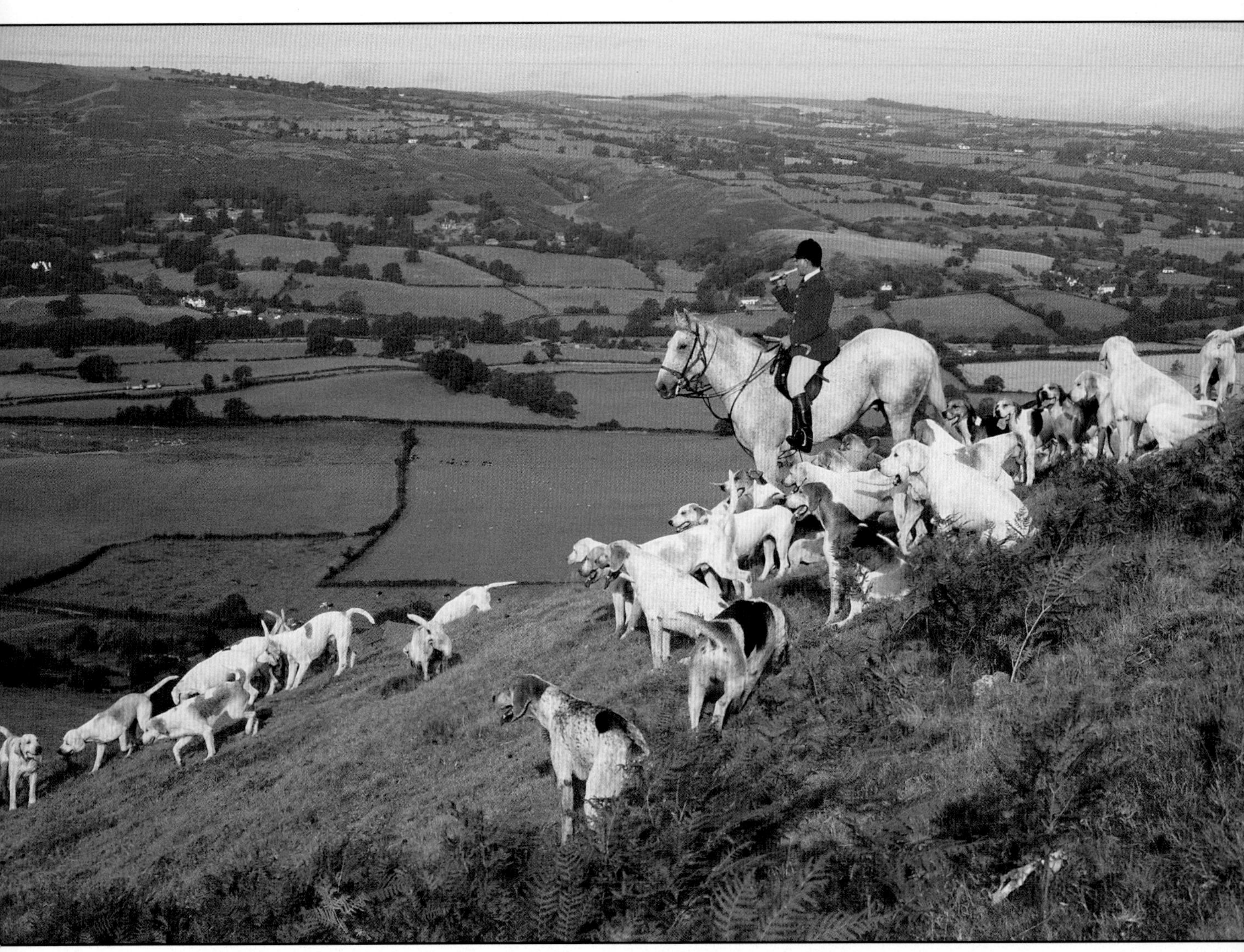

Michael Rowson, who hunted the South Shropshire hounds for 30 years, collecting his good looking pack on a steep grassy hillside at the end of a morning of autumn hunting in the Church Stretton area.

S

The STAFFORDSHIRE MOORLAND *Hunt*

Field master of the Staffordshire Moorland Hunt, Val Turner, heading a group of galloping riders during a hunt amidst marvellous open country.

The end of the day for the Staffordshire Moorland Hunt as they head for home behind huntsman Paul Goddard and his whipper-in wife Judith.

S

Mr STEWART'S CHESHIRE *Hunt* (UNITED STATES OF AMERICA)

Mrs Nancy Hannum, master of Mr Stewart's Cheshire foxhounds since 1945, here with son Jock at a meet near Unionville, Pennsylvania, USA. For a great number of years, Mrs Hannum hunted these hounds in a most professional way and with much success.

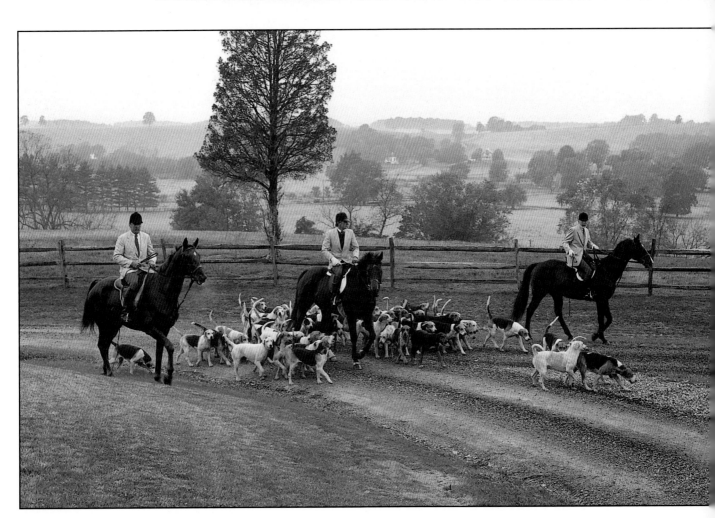

Huntsman to Mr Stewart's Cheshire foxhounds Joseph Cassidy, bringing hounds to a frosty meet near Unionville, Pennsylvania. Flanking him are whippers-in Mark Cassidy and Monk Crossan.

The East SUSSEX AND ROMNEY MARSH *Hunt*

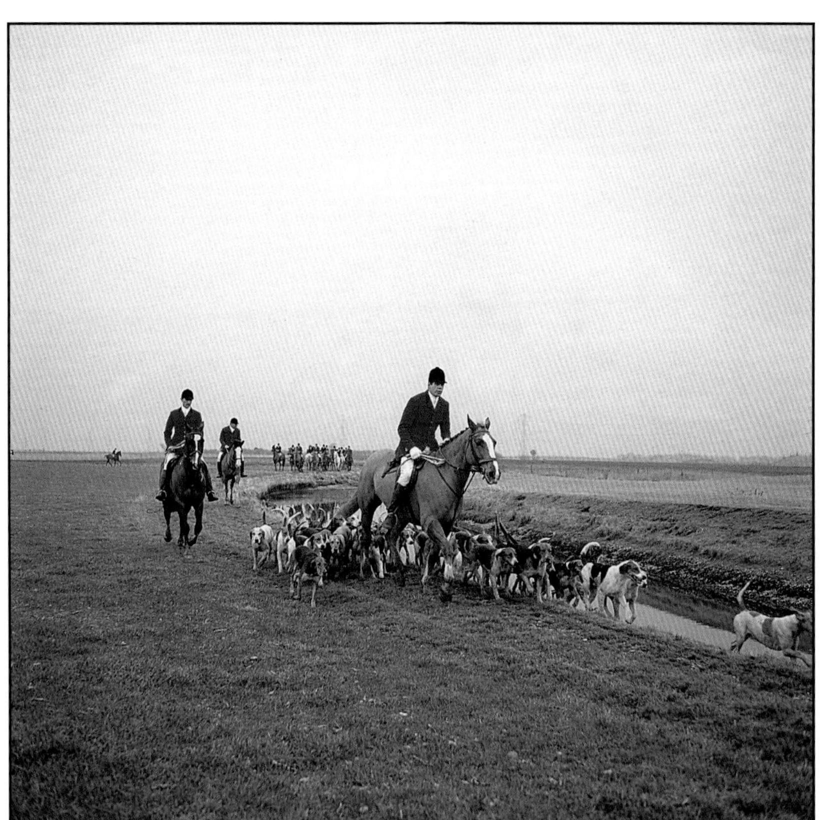

Following the banks of a meandering water course across Romney Marsh are huntsman Godfrey Berry and hounds on their way to draw a field of kale.

The East Sussex and Romney Marsh foxhounds, led by huntsman Godfrey Berry, moving along a shingle beach on the English Channel coast.

T

The
TEME VALLEY
Hunt
(WELSH BORDERS)

With overnight snow coating the hill tops on the Welsh/English border, huntsman Roy Savage takes his mixed pack of fell and Welsh hounds to a fresh draw.

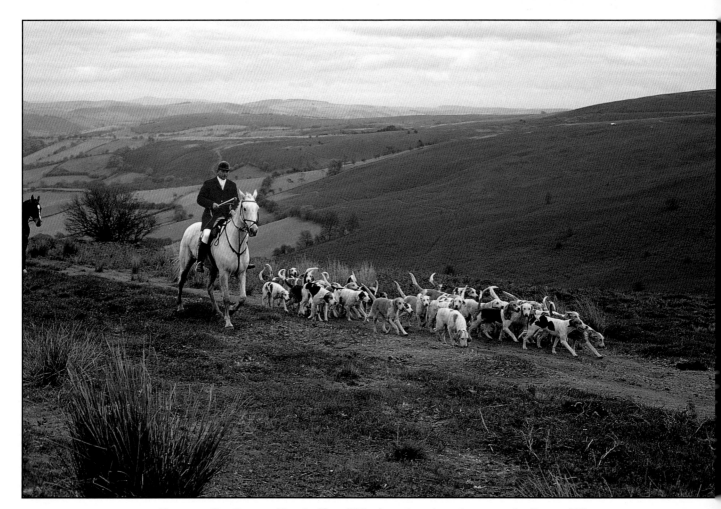

Huntsman Roy Savage taking the Teme Valley hounds to draw the spectacular Beacon Hill, where the heather clad summit is on the 1800 foot contour, and where the foxes are big and strong running.

TERRIERS

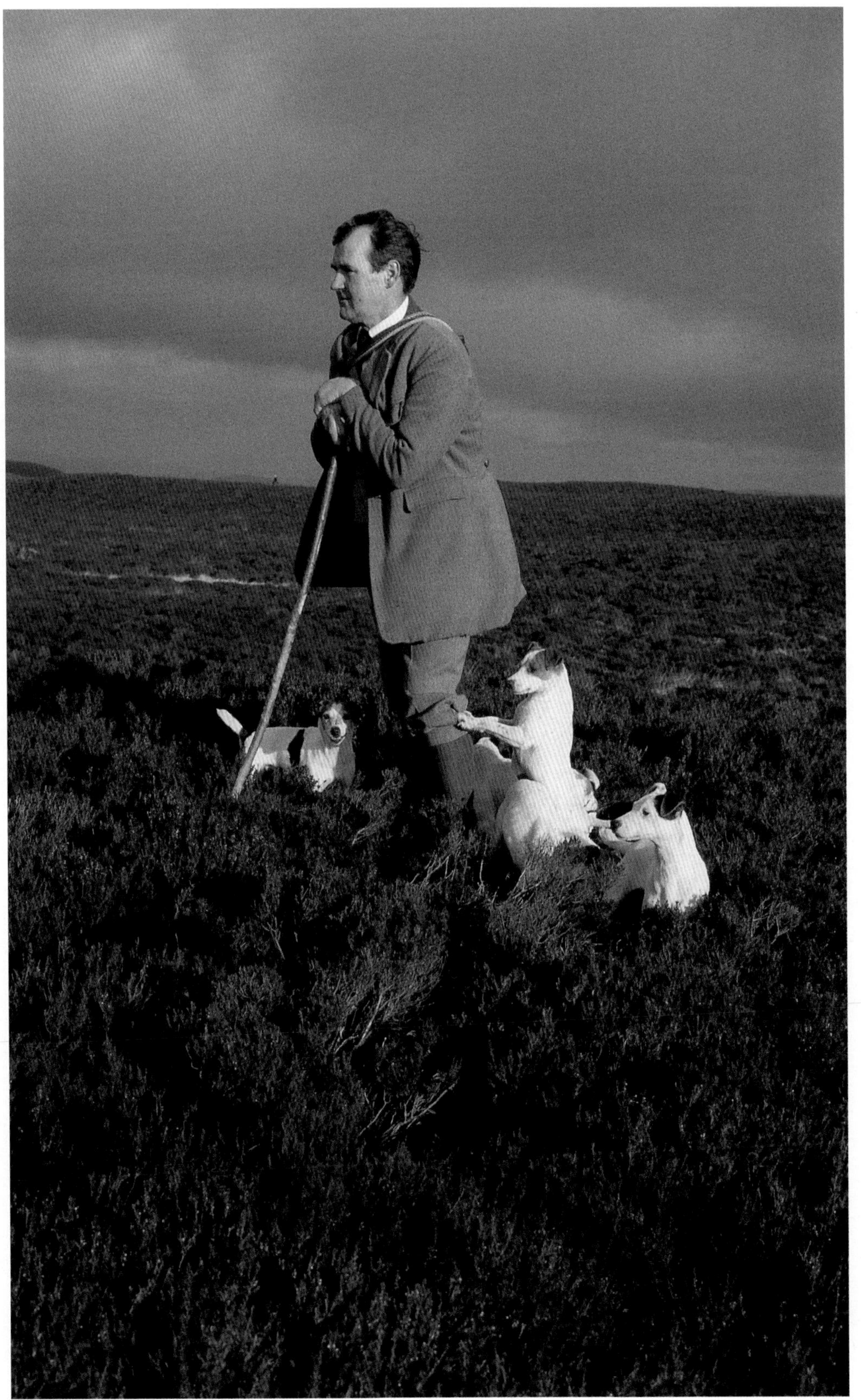

Terriers are an integral part of foxhunting and some of the best are bred by David Davies huntsman David Jones, seen here with a group during a day's foot hunting on the heather. Many of his terriers have crossed the Atlantic, where they win numerous prizes at the major summer shows in America.

TIGER TRAPS

Lord Daresbury, MFH Sir Watkin Williams-Wynn's Hunt, is a former top steeplechase rider and champion point-to-point rider. He is now chairman of the Masters of Foxhounds Association.

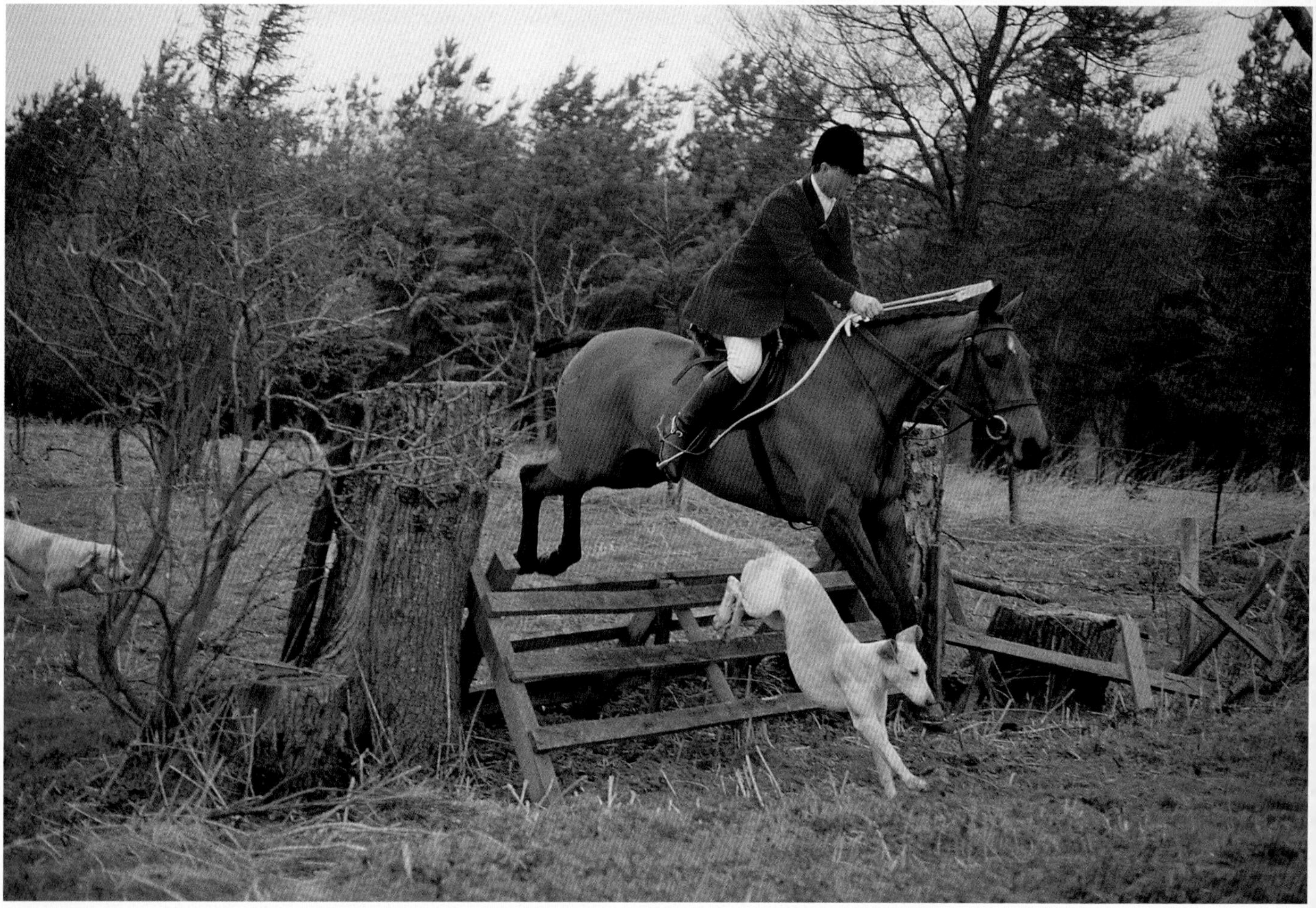

Fitzwilliam huntsman George Adams going away from a covert, with hounds.

TIMBER

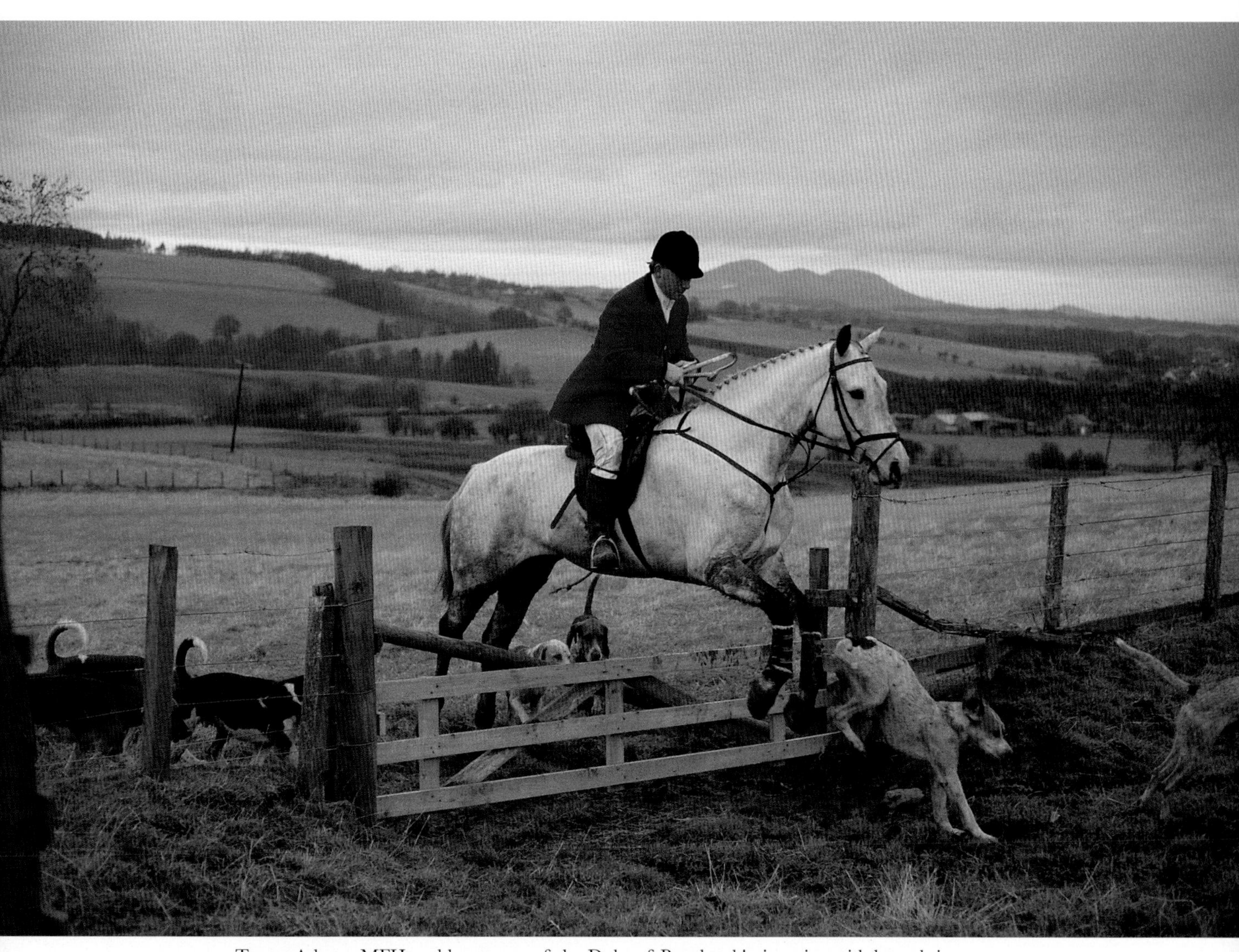

Trevor Adams, MFH and huntsman of the Duke of Buccleuch's, jumping with hounds in sheep country.

T

TIMBER

Joint master of the Sinnington Hunt, Andrew Osborne, over timber set in barbed wire.

TIMBER

Jumping a typical Pennsylvania post and rails fence near Unionville is Beth Clark Lamont.

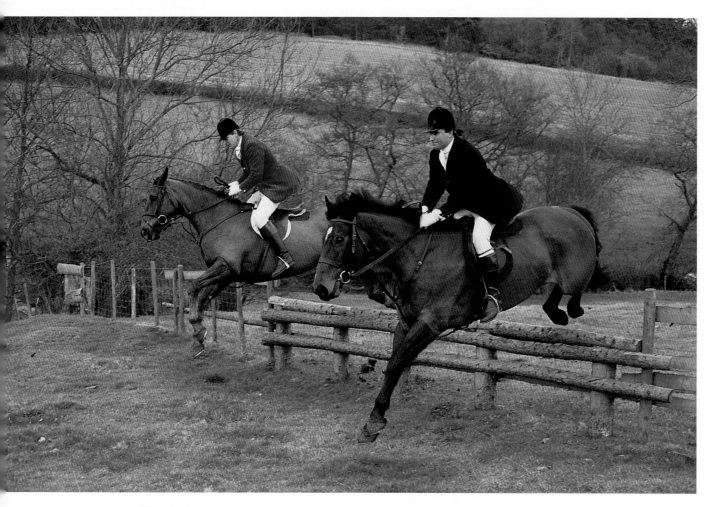

Kim Cockburn and Brian Perry, in hot pursuit of the Warwickshire hounds.

T

The
TIPPERARY
Hunt
(IRELAND)

Tipperary joint master Timmy Hyde clearing an Irish bank and ditch during a hunt from Rosegreen. Mr Hyde is well known on both sides of the Atlantic as a knowledgeable bloodstock agent.

Against a panorama of delectable grass country, Tipperary huntsman Simon Probin takes his top-class pack of hounds to a fresh draw.

The TORONTO AND NORTH YORK *Hunt* (CANADA)

The Toronto and North York hunt, led by huntsman Mark Powell, moving off from a meet at their club house, near Newmarket in Canada.

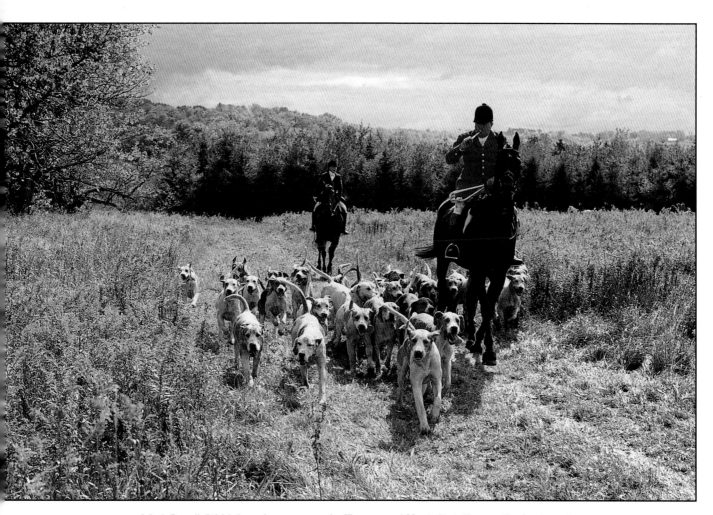

Mark Powell, Welsh born huntsman to the Toronto and North York Hunt, collecting hounds at the end of a good hunt. Following is his whipper-in wife Emma, who also comes from Wales.

The
TRYON
Hunt
(UNITED STATES OF AMERICA)

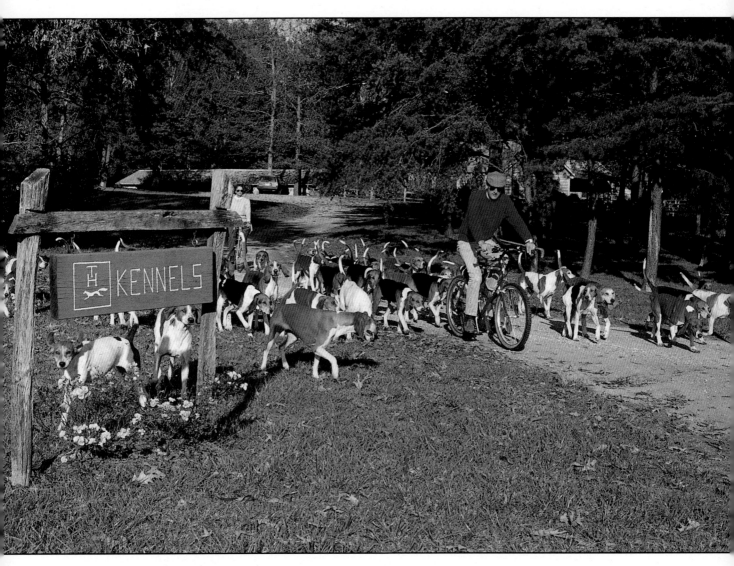

Bob Ashcom, joint master and huntsman of the Tryon hounds, is one of the few in America who exercise hounds on bicycles. Following is his wife Susie, who helps with the duties of whipper-in.

The UNITED *Hunt* (WELSH BORDERS)

The United pack, with joint master and huntsman Mark Hankinson and kennel-huntsman Nick Wilson, moving off from an early morning meet at Lower Down, Lydbury North.

With white mist cloaking the low ground, the United pack and hunt staff are lit by an early morning sun, as they move across old turf on their way to draw a covert near Lydbury North.

The VALE OF CLETTWR *Hunt* (WEST WALES)

With her pack of Welsh foxhounds and surrounded by numerous keen foot-followers is Elizabeth Thorneycroft MFH. This meet, as are so many others, was held at a local public house which offered a warming stirrup cup to start the day.

Elizabeth Thorneycroft, the first lady joint master in the history of the Vale of Clettwr Hunt, taking hounds to draw, during the season when she carried the horn after the huntsman and joint master Lyn Lloyd was injured.

V

The

VALE OF LUNE HARRIERS

(LANCASHIRE AND YORKSHIRE)

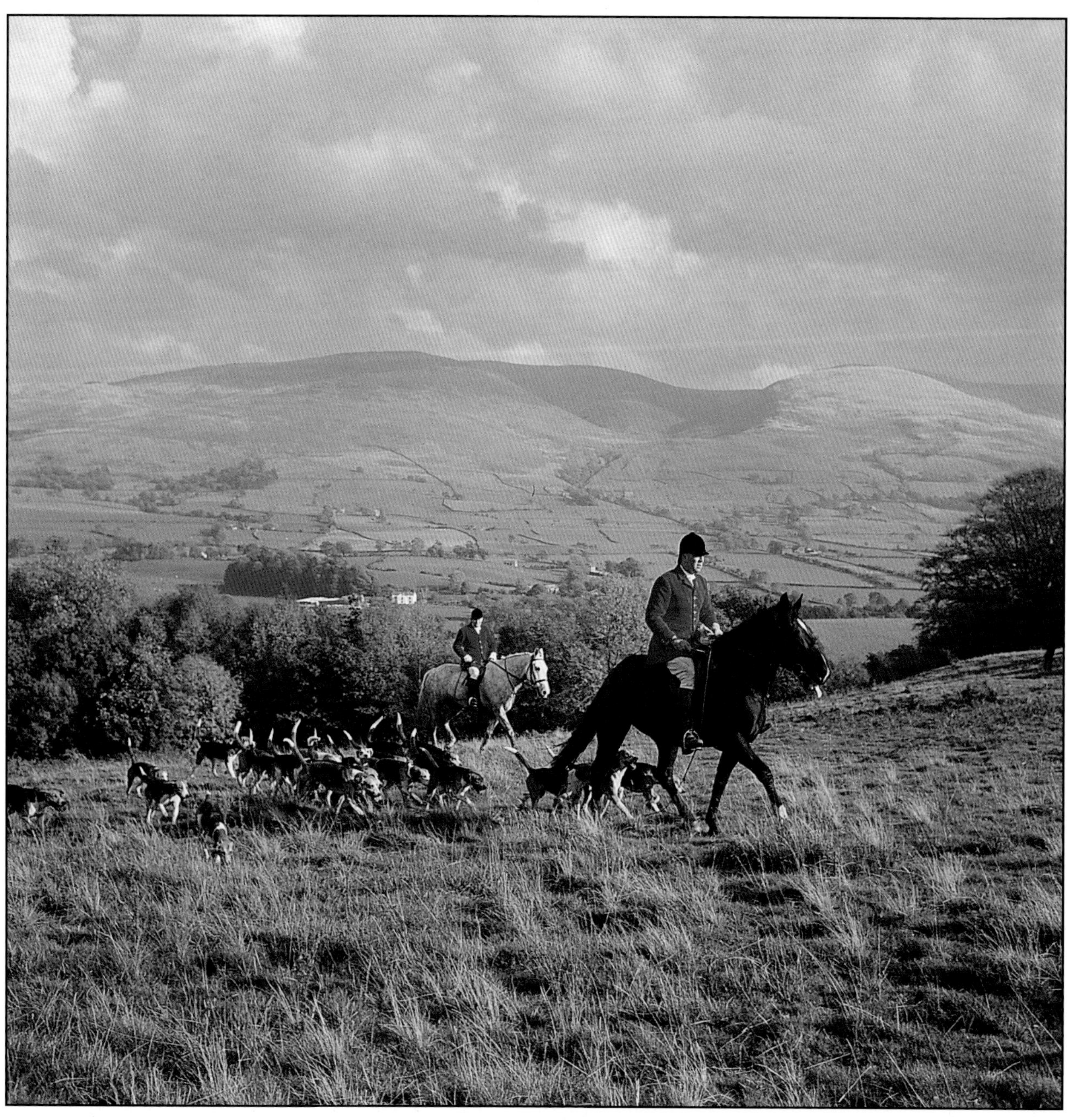

The Vale of Lune Harriers, with huntsman David Reed, in spectacularly beautiful country on the Lancashire, Yorkshire borders, in north-west England. This is one of very few packs of harriers where the hunt staff wear scarlet coats.

V

The VALE OF WHITE HORSE *Hunt* (Wiltshire and Gloucestershire)

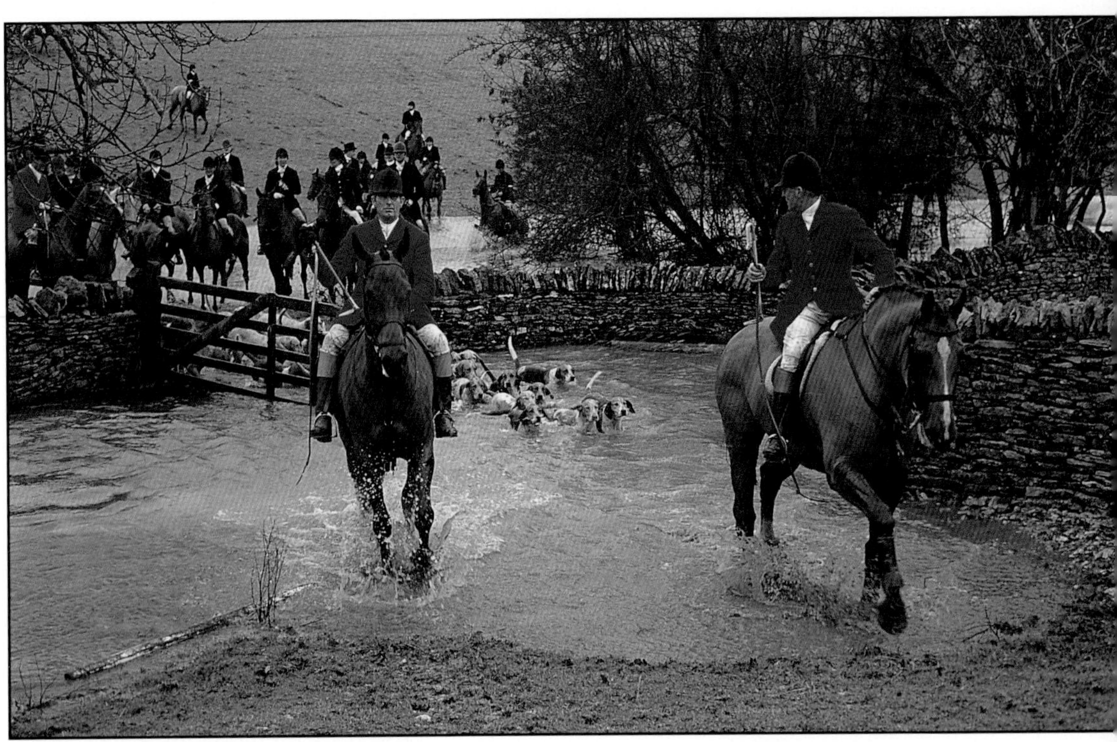

Following a very wet spell of weather, Sidney Bailey and Michael Farrin bringing hounds and riders through flood water from a swollen stream on their way to change horses.

Vale of White Horse huntsman since 1966, Sidney Bailey, and Quorn huntsman for 30 seasons, Michael Farrin, leading hounds and a huge mounted field from a joint meet at Aldsworth, Gloucestershire.

WALLS

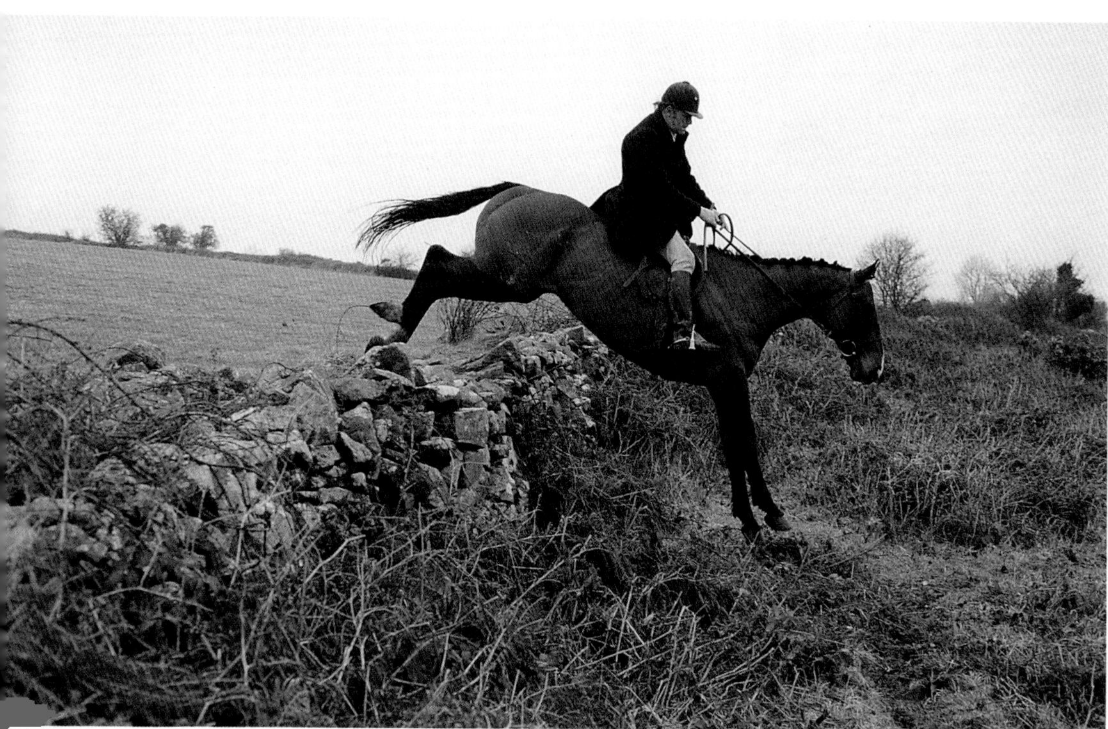

Jumping into bracken, in County Kilkenny, is Michael Mains with the Kilkenny Hunt.

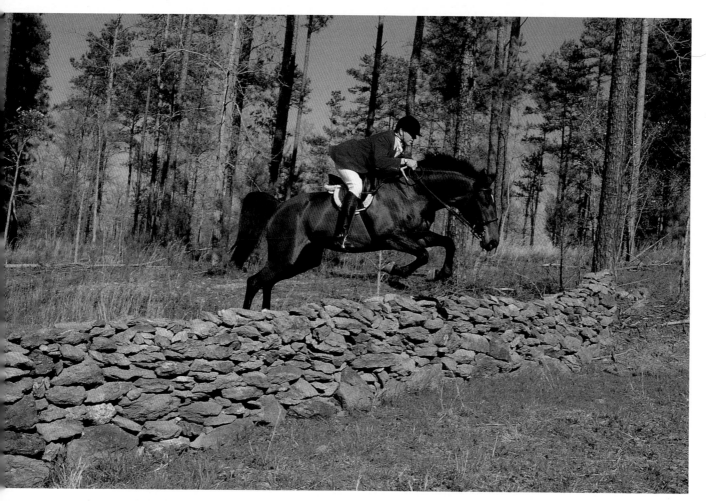

Stylishly clearing this stone wall in Georgia USA is 'Epp' Wilson, joint master and huntsman of the Belle Meade Hunt.

WALLS

Over a typical Derbyshire wall is Linda Jenkins-Good, an American who was a joint master of the High Peak Harriers. She now hunts with the Blue Ridge hounds in Virginia, USA.

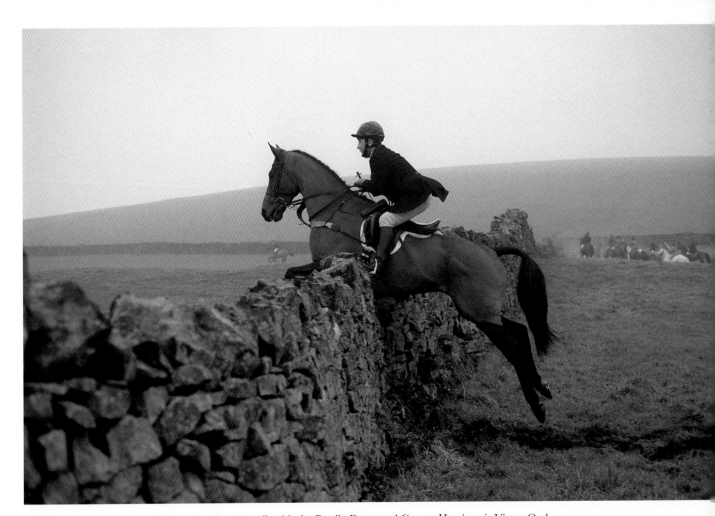

Over a good stone wall, with the Pendle Forest and Craven Harriers, is Victor Ogden.

WALLS

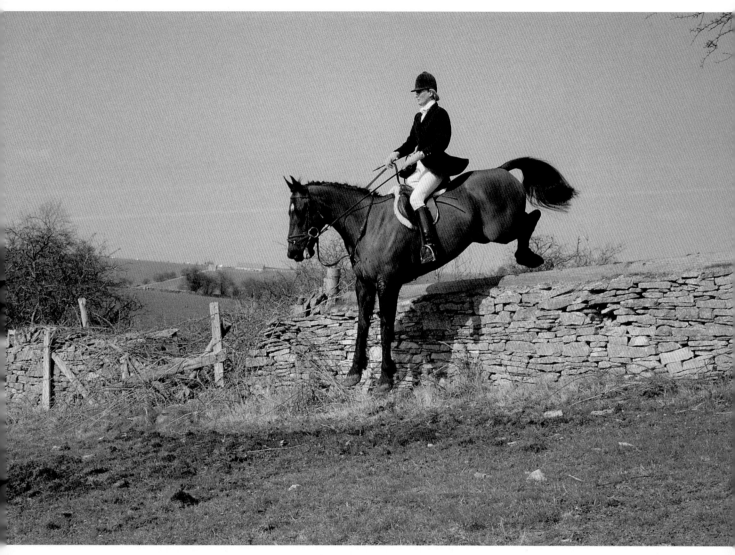

The Hon Judith Strutt elegantly clears a Heythrop wall, with a drop.

WALLS

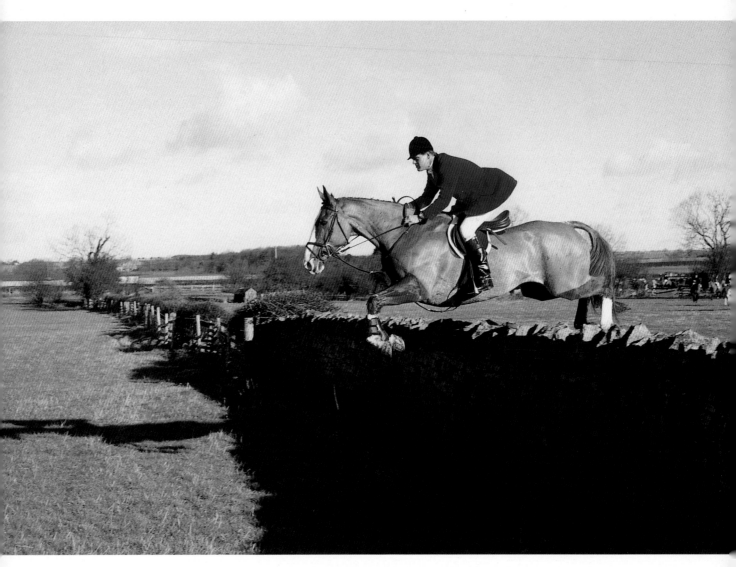

Well over a big stone wall in the Zetland country is joint master Paul Morrison, who is also field master.

WALLS WI
TIMBE

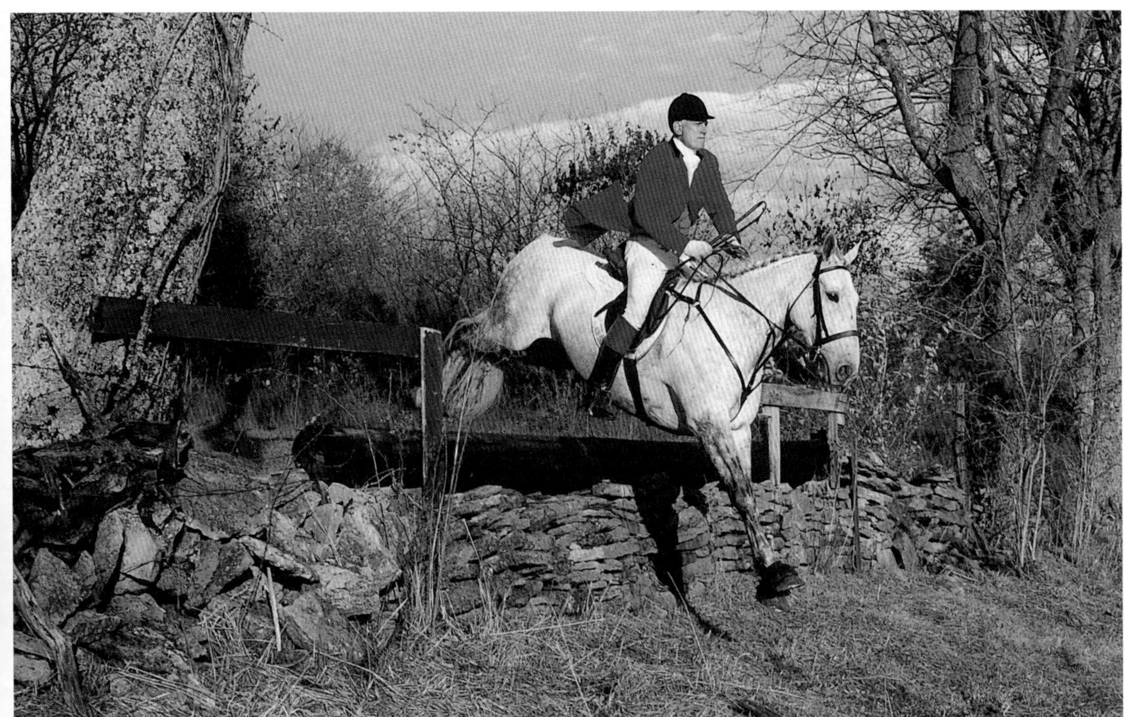

Iroquois Hunt joint master Dr Jack van Nagell well over a Kentucky stone wall, topped with timber, as he leaves 'The Jungle' covert.

Two joint masters of the VWH Hunt, Norman Thomas and John Phillips, leading the field.

Bethan Jones and her pony make nothing of this wall, in the David Davies hill country.

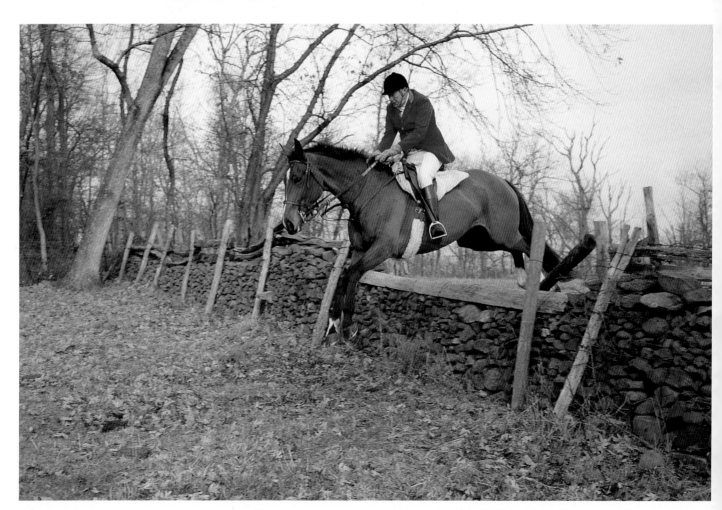

Heading the hunt over a Virginia wall with timber is Ben Hardaway III MFH Midland hounds since 1950.

WALLS WITH TIMBER

Sue Gosling takes this wall with timber in her stride, during a hunt in open country with the Staffordshire Moorland Hunt.

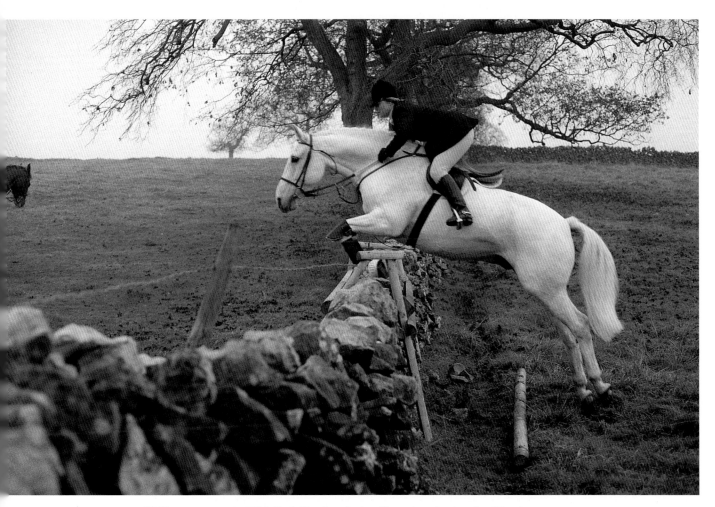

Field secretary to the High Peak Harriers, Janine Noon, jumping in splendid style.

WARE WIRE!

Monmouthshire huntsman Norman Stubbings gives a wire fence plenty of clearance, during a fast hunt.

Roy Tatlow, master and huntsman of the Clifton on Teme Hunt, clearing a new, tall wire fence in order to keep with hounds on his very last day as master and huntsman! – 6 March 1999.

The WARWICKSHIRE *Hunt*

Warwickshire huntsman William Deakin bringing hounds to an invitation meet at Downton Hall, home of Micky Wiggin in the Ludlow country, where they produced an excellent day's hunting.

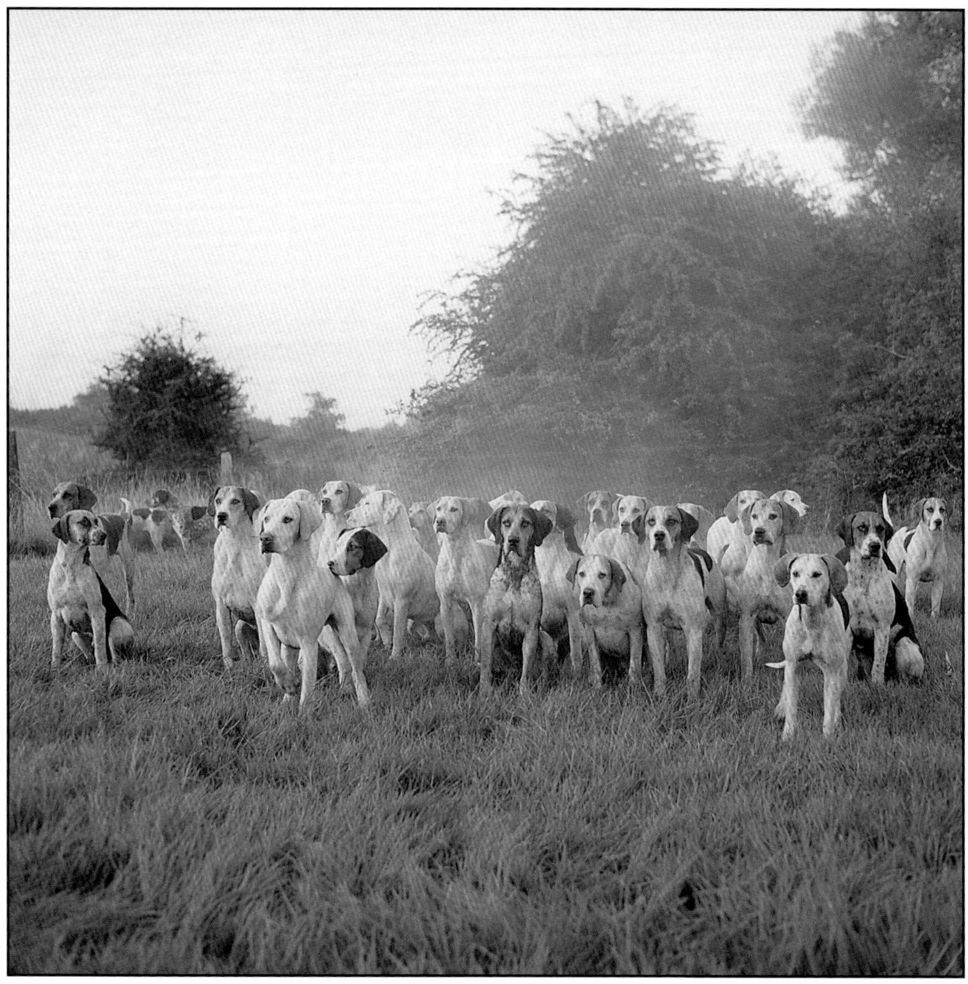

The Warwickshire pack, watching and waiting, after marking a fox to ground during autumn hunting.

W

Sir
WATKIN WILLIAMS-WYNN'S
Hunt
(WELSH BORDERS)

Heading the field of Sir Watkin Williams-Wynn's Hunt on a grassy hillside, as they climb out of a deep valley, are Lord Daresbury MFH, Sir Jonathan Clark and Caroline Jenks.

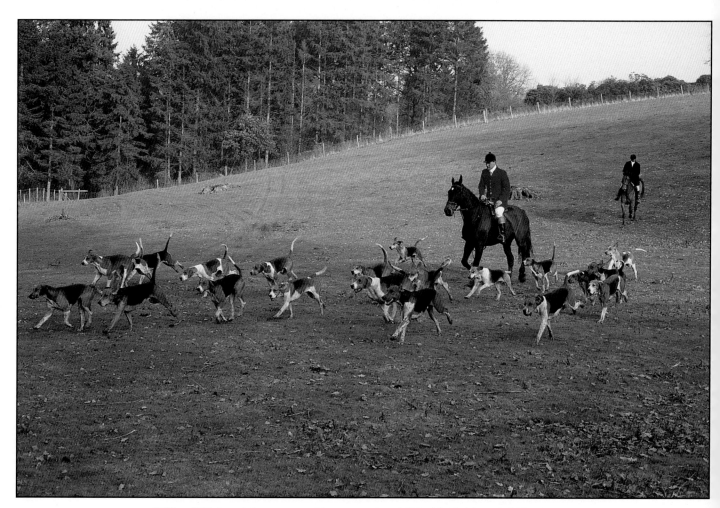

William Wakeham joint master and huntsman since 1998 with his 'almost' old English hounds on lovely old turf from a meet at Gredington.

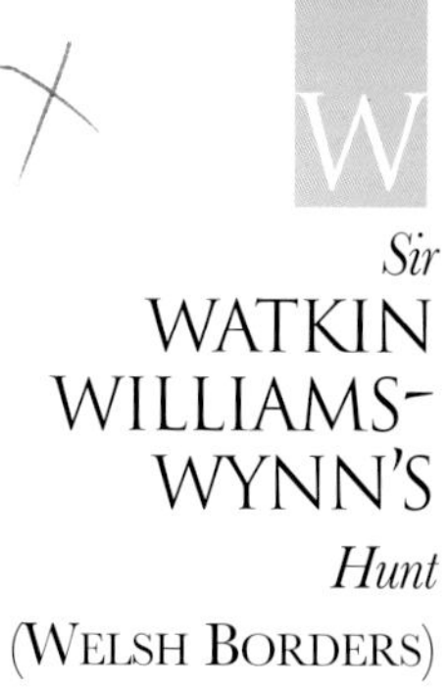

Sir WATKIN WILLIAMS-WYNN'S *Hunt*

(WELSH BORDERS)

In his first season as joint master and huntsman, William Wakeham gives this timber fence plenty of clearance as he takes hounds to a 'Holloa'.

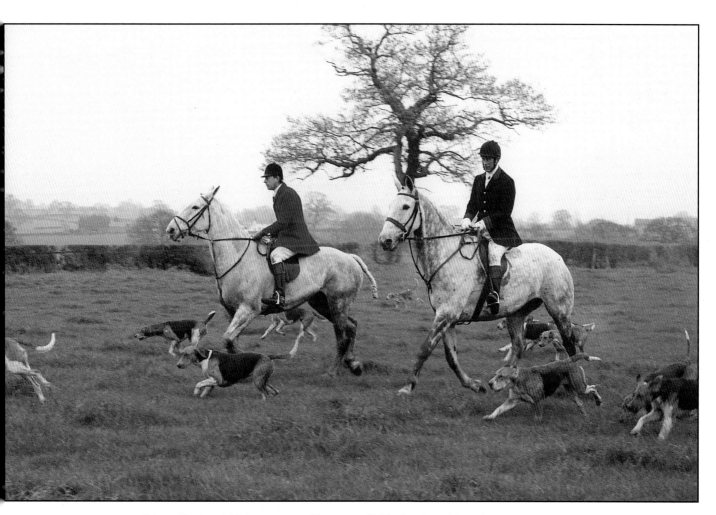

Prince Charles and joint master and huntsman Robin Gundry, with the Wynnstay hounds during a wet day's hunting.

The WEARDALE AND TEES VALLEY BEAGLES

After one successful hunt, professional huntsman Stephen Batchelor and joint master Angus Thompson take hounds to draw again through an area of burned heather.

This photo of the Weardale and Tees Valley beagles in full cry, high on a heather covered hill, made all the sweat expended in getting to the right place, at the right time, very worth while!

WASHING OFF

Washing off their horses at the end of a very muddy day with the Meynell Hunt are Helen Connors, Etta Madocks-Wright, Nick Connors and Caroline Hodges (now Mrs Henry Coke).

Followers of the South Pembrokeshire Hunt washing off their horses in the river at Cresswell Quay after a busy day's foxhunting in West Wales.